COWBOY TALES ALONG THE TRAIL

JACK TERRY

HARVEST HOUSE PUBLISHERS
EUGENE, OREGON

> Art Trends Fine Art & Licensing
> 1-800-223-5020; 931-261-8956
> www.arttrendsfineart.com

Cover design by Koechel Peterson & Associates, Inc., Minneapolis, Minnesota

COWBOY TALES ALONG THE TRAIL
Previously published as Harvest House gift books with artwork by Jack Terry: *Wide Open Spaces* (2004), *Prayers Along the Trail* (2003), *A Cowboy's Faith* (2001), and *The Great Trail Ride* (2000)
Text copyright © 2012/2004/2003/2001/2000 by Jack Terry
Published by Harvest House Publishers
Eugene, Oregon 97402
www.harvesthousepublishers.com

Library of Congress Cataloging-in-Publication Data
Terry, Jack.
  Cowboy tales along the trail / Jack Terry.
    p. cm.
  ISBN 978-0-7369-4581-3 (pbk.)
  ISBN 978-0-7369-4582-0 (eBook)
  1. Cowboys—Religious life. I. Title.
  BV4596.C65T464 2012
  242'.68—dc23

                                                        2012007744

Printed in the United States of America

12 13 14 15 16 17 18 19 20 / VP-CD / 10 9 8 7 6 5 4 3 2 1

To my grandparents
Bill and Maggie Mason and R.L. and Etna Terry.
They were pioneers into the West, and
their lives of hardship, dedication, and faith
helped shape generations.

To my parents, Frank and Della Herring,
who have been my lifelong
encouragers, supporters, and fans.

And especially to my wife, Anita,
who keeps the fire in my heart burning to
always be the very best I can be.
I love you.

Acknowledgment

My thanks to Harvest House Publishers. You have given me a decade of opportunities to share my stories and paintings. Thank you for your love and dedication to the gospel.

CONTENTS

Are There Any Heroes Today?

L ife. Why are we here? What are we doing and where are we going? The mystery of our being, the necessity of our actions, the dependence of all things upon the other, the magnitude and beauty of creation itself, and our desire to know the answers to these mysteries assures each of us that life has a specific purpose that everything points to.

The psalmist David wrote, "You will make known to me the path of life; in Your presence is fullness of joy; in Your right hand there are pleasures forever" (Psalm 16:11 NASB). Everyone wants to experience joy and happiness on the trail ride of life. As a cowboy controls the movements of his horse with a bridle, the trails of our lives must be guided by this wisdom: "Your word is a lamp to my feet and a light to my path" (Psalm 119:105 NASB). God has not only given us His Word to guide us, but His Spirit to lead us and prayer to communicate with Him while on this great trail ride of life.

I was initially guided down that path riding in the saddle with my grandfather on the bay horse we called Old Dan. Granddad was a working cowboy from the early age of 13, and he rode on some of the last great cattle drives from Texas to the northern railheads. He ingrained in me the code of ethics that the hero known as the "American cowboy" adhered to. I listened to stories of business transactions and trades completed with mere handshakes. A man's word was his bond. I learned firsthand of the rewards of a loving family guided by principles of faith, responsibility, honesty, and integrity.

My other granddad was a jack of all trades, living on his own and surviving alone in a cave in West Texas while still a child himself. In his later years, when I was just an early teen, he was a true inspiration and reminder to me that "with God all things are possible" (Matthew 19:26). No matter how bad the drought that devastated his business or how painful the disease that claimed the life of one of his young children, Granddad always kept his faith in God. Prayer always saw him and his family through life's most troubling times.

Now, my granddads were not the most educated and eloquent individuals, as was true of most cowboys of that era. But they knew that life had a purpose directly linked to their relationship with their Maker. This wasn't something to be discovered from fortune, power, or personal fame. They believed we are all put here to be caretakers of God's creation, stewards of the land, livestock, and people we love. They also believed we are to enjoy life and have a little fun while we're here. A little hunting and fishing, a good rodeo, and a ball game were always welcome.

Both of my granddads would be the first to tell you that it was their wives, my grandmothers, who led them to church and kept them there. My earliest memories of these great pioneering women are best summed up by Proverbs 31:26-29: "She speaks with wisdom, and faithful instruction is on her tongue. She watches over the affairs of her household and does not eat the bread of idleness. Her children arise and call her blessed; her husband also, and he praises her: 'Many women do noble things, but you surpass them all.'" What a wonderful heritage I have enjoyed! These great women were the mortar that held our family together through many hard times and who fed, taught, and encouraged generations.

My family was always known for loving the outdoors, whether it was pushin' cattle along a dusty trail or baiting a hook to land a big one from a nearby stock tank or river. I grew up knowing and loving the outdoors and the cowboy way of life. Many folks understand the spirit of the cowboy even though they may know little of his actual profession. Nature has a way of blending the majesty and beauty of God's great creation into a language everyone can understand if he or she will only take the time to listen and observe. There are many who enjoy fly-fishing for trout or chasing giant redfish in the Gulf of Mexico, who pursue the great sailfish in the ocean or the mighty bull elk atop a snow-covered mountaintop. While I enjoy so many of these activities and sports as well, the blood of the cowboy runs deep in my veins. Often I find myself lost in dreams of being a cowboy— a true cowboy.

Real Cowboys

FARMING

What do I mean by a real cowboy? The man who rode his horse through every kind of weather and whose bed was usually the hard, rocky ground. His favorite place to be was atop his cowpony along a dusty trail. The one who lived every day depending on the hand of the Lord to go before him and provide food and water for the cattle and safety and provision for his days in the saddle. The person who rode with the herd from the deserts in South Texas to the mountaintops in Wyoming, and who trusted God for all things—whether it was fish from the river, deer from the hillsides, or a dry piece of jerky in his saddlebag that tasted like manna from heaven. There is a great lesson for us all in that simple trust and dependence on God for all things.

Yes, cowboy blood runs deep in my family. There are few real-life cowboys today, but there are many who share the love and beauty of creation all over the earth, just as the cowboy did. It is no wonder the American cowboy is so revered throughout the world. Simple men, honorable men, humble men who sat in a saddle and cared for their families, livestock, and the land they called home. I am so very thankful that the blood of Jesus ran deep through the veins of my grandfathers, and that love was passed down to me.

> Happiness is inward, and not outward; and so it does not depend on what we have, but on what we are.
>
> HENRY VAN DYKE

Many times the cowboy was viewed as being a loner, when in actuality he was a team player. Each man was an integral part of a unifying operation with a specific job to do and the talents necessary for success in the West. On a typical cattle drive from South Texas to Kansas, the trail boss would generally ride in front of the herd. He would take breaks from the front position and ride back to talk to some of the other cowboys during different times of the day to check on the herd and make plans for resting the cattle that evening.

Behind the trail boss usually came the chuck wagon loaded with cowboy bedrolls and provisions. To the side of the chuck wagon was the remuda, additional horses needed by the cowboys, led by a wrangler. Behind the chuck wagon, cowboys known as "point riders" led the beginning of the herd down the trail each day, keeping them calm and focused on the path ahead. Often with a whistle, a call, or a yodel, they would lure the lead steer along calmly. That usually older and calmer steer wore a bell around his neck that all the other cows could hear and follow.

As the multitude of cattle began to stretch out behind the leaders, cowboys known as "swing riders" rode along the sides to keep the cattle moving forward toward the leaders. The weaker cattle and those with babies moved slower and lagged yet farther behind. They were urged on by "flank riders" on each side. The worst cow-pushin' job of all was that of being "drag riders." There were usually three to five young, usually first-time on the trail cowboys, whose job it was to keep all the cattle moving, working with the sickest and weakest at the rear of the herd. No matter how hot and tired they were, everyone had a specific job and a designated position in the drive, and each cowboy was essential to the success of the long journey. They had to be a unified team with faith and confidence in each other to see the job through successfully.

The Cowboy Spirit in Christian Life Today

It was crucial that the cowboys work as one orderly team as they pushed several thousand head of stubborn cattle for many perilous months along the trail to their destination. When trouble came, those cowboys had to operate as one unit. Each man had a separate but specifically crucial job whether he was trail boss in the front or eatin' dust as a drag rider.

First Corinthians 12:14-20 describes God's order for His church and the guiding principle of life for each of us:

The body is not made up of one part but of many. Now if the foot should say, "Because I am not a hand, I do not belong to the body," it would not for that reason stop being part of the body. And if the ear should say, "Because I am not an eye, I do not belong to the body," it would not for that reason stop being part of the body. If the whole body were an eye, where would the sense of hearing be? If the whole body were an ear, where would the sense of smell be? But in fact God has placed the parts in the body, every one of them, just as he wanted them to be. If they were all one part, where would the body be? As it is, there are many parts, but one body.

Such was the life of the cattle-driving cowboy, and such is the life of the individual member of the church.

As members of Christ's church, we must accept the responsibility of our great calling and utilize our positions and giftings to watch over "the herd" and lead the lost and wandering to their final destination—eternal life with Christ. When a cowboy signed on to complete a cattle drive and agreed to the pay he was due when the job was completed, he knew it was necessary to fill his position with pride and utilize all his skills to the best of his ability. He understood what it was to be a team member and carry his own weight, even while depending on and deferring to the strength of his team members when necessary or when he couldn't perform at his very best.

There are many of us in our country and worldwide who love the cowboy and his way of life. Because of my wonderful family history and personal opportunities for relationships with great cowboys, world champion rodeo participants, great country singers and songwriters, actors, and even a "cowboy" in the White House (George W. Bush), I have grown up with a great respect for these true American heroes. The truth of the matter is there are very few true cowboys left—in the Old West sense of the word. I'm talking handfuls across America.

These uniquely gifted, rugged, simple individuals know they aren't placed on this great earth to *be* somebody but to pursue the desires of their hearts. They know they are men (and women) with a special fire in their hearts to be who God made them to be—and do it with honor, integrity, and grace. I know that while the lives they live may be different from mine, we share a common thread. We who accept the goodness of God's grace have the invitation to follow our hearts and be instruments of encouragement and change. Maybe we have what it takes to be heroes as well.

Finding and Being Heroes for God

While it is not absolutely necessary here on earth, it sure helps as an encouragement through the challenges of this life to be able to wrap our arms around a real, live hero. The Lord provides the way for the meek and humble to be heroes and to move from last to first in His kingdom. The challenge is to observe our past and present to find these men and women of honor. Who has influenced our lives and hearts for the good? How have we applied their wisdom and skills to perpetuate God's love? Even more importantly than that is to appreciate the uniqueness of every individual and to encourage others to find their purpose and put their God-given talents and gifts in motion. This is the stuff heroes are made of.

Some of the great heroes and encouragers in my life go hundreds of years back in history. Some have been young cowboys riding the open range and surviving perilous years of drought, disease, and hardship. They married at very young ages and quickly grew into mature men and women out of necessity. They needed each other to survive, and they raised families who ranched and farmed and fought for the freedom and survival of this great country in every war we have fought since 1776. My family history is filled with heroes. Two uncles were prisoners of war in World War II, another was wounded and sent home with a Purple Heart, and yet another relative was killed defending the Alamo. Many others sacrificed so that we can enjoy our freedom. My earliest American descendent, my great-great-great-grandfather, William Whipple, signed the Declaration of Independence. From an attorney who helped found this nation to a couple of worn-out West Texas cattle pushers, from heroes in uniform defending our freedom to parents who sacrificed and provided, I have known a lot of heroes. Sure, they all had faults and weaknesses, but they gave life their best shot and left many great memories and examples for me and future generations.

Our founding fathers intended for our republic to be guided by the principles of God, one nation indivisible. A place where everyone has the opportunity to be a hero by having the freedom to follow the path God put before him or her. No matter our backgrounds or stories, the common thread we have running through us as believers is best summed up by Jeremiah 29:11-13: "'For I know the plans I have for you,' declares the LORD, 'plans to prosper you and not to harm you, plans to give you hope and a future.'" We are all blessed knowing God has a plan for us to prosper, and we have been put on this earth for a reason. We are promised hope and a future—and that's the stuff heroes are made of.

The Lord wants each of us to have an abundant life. One that is happy and where we make a difference in the lives of others. He wants us to be life-changers through lives that reflect His glory.

> The pioneers and ranchers of the frontier would never have made the West habitable had it not been for these wild cowboys, these...hard-riding, hard-living rangers of the barrens, these easy, cool, laconic, simple young men whose blood was tinged with fire and who possessed a magnificent and terrible effrontery toward danger and death.
>
> ZANE GREY, *The Man of the Forest*

He wants us to be great heroes of faith to shine the way for people to come to Him.

Now that so many years have passed and I am a grandfather, I am finally coming to understand the true role of heroes in our lives. I pray you delight as I do in the one and only true Hero who never disappoints and never fails. Jesus desires to be everyone's Hero. With so many needs in our families and those suffering throughout the world, let's welcome Him into our lives. Let's take God at His Word and invite Him to be everything we need. Let's allow Him to use us to reach out to the people around us with His honesty, integrity, and love.

Part 1

THE GREAT TRAIL RIDE

JUST A COWBOY

Lord, I'm just a cowboy
Like my granddad who's gone away
I'm really not a loner
Folks just look at me that way.

My life is one of pleasure
I love the work I do
I know I'm special in Your eyes
'Cause I'm made in the image of You.

You brought me into this world
Like a newborn calf in the spring
My legs were wobbly and my eyes were bright
And Your voice in my ears did ring.

You grew me up in this land that I love
With family and friends so true
Showed me the greatness of Your creation
From magnificent vistas and views.

With a good, stout horse between my knees
Down many trails I did ride
Some were rocky and many were steep
But You were always right there by my side.

Like the time we were in Whisper Valley
Drivin' longhorns from daybreak till dusk
The cool mornin' breeze blew through the great bluffs
As hawks soared in the clouds up above.

We herded those cows across the great creek
And up the steep hills high and wide
Through grass lush and green and rocks big as trees
And hot sun beaten' down on their hide.

We rested at lunch in the chuck wagon's shade
Ate biscuits and gravy and steak
We caught a few winks and swapped a few tales
Then tracks for the trail we did make.

We rode hard and fast through canyons and rocks
Where some of us stumbled and fell
Then climbed the great mountain where camp was set up
With a campfire and stories to tell.

The full moon was risin' in the night sky above
As I lay in my bedroll on the ground
The stars were so bright, what a glorious sight
The silence was deafening, not a sound.

Save for the whistle of a hawk on the wing
And an occasional coyote yell
I drifted to sleep in a slumber so deep
It seems You had a story to tell.

"I am the Lord, I've been with you all day
I'm the sun and the moon and the stars

I'm the water and grass and the birds in the sky
I love you, My son, 'twas for you that I died.

"Like your granddad before you, I'm there when you fall
When you stumble while riding life's trail
I'll pick you up and guide you each day
You'll help others with the story you tell."

When the new day had dawned, I remembered my dream
And I thought of the streets paved with gold
Where my loved ones have gone and wait there for me
I reflected on the story God told.

But wait, I'm a cowboy
With lots of work yet to do
The coffee is ready and the cows are awaitin'
And the trail boss is callin' me too.

So for now, Lord, just let me ride on the trails of this life
Till my job on earth here is through
'Cause I'm as close to heaven as I'll ever be
Till I ride that great trail home to You.

Character:
There's One in Every Bunch

Some years back I spent a week on one of the oldest and largest ranches in West Texas rounding up cattle during the fall. The first pasture we worked was about 25,000 acres under one fence. The terrain is very mountainous with large rolling plateaus and deep canyons. The ranch foreman instructed us early the first morning that we were to look for and gather about 850 mother cows, many with calves that were scattered throughout the pastures.

This experience was truly stepping back into what life was probably like 100 years ago for the American cowboy. We rode out from the ranch headquarters at first light accompanied by a chuck wagon loaded with provisions for our six-day roundup. The plan was to arrive at our destination about four hours down the trail and set up our camp. I noticed that the other four cowboys kept watching every move I made out of the corner of their eyes, even though they never said a word to me. I realized at that point they thought of me as a city slicker and intended to have some laughs at my expense. When you're all alone in the middle of thousands of acres with nothing but your saddle, slicker, and bedroll, you feel rather insignificant.

I knew it was time to make a friend. Ramón was in charge of the chuck wagon and preparing all of our meals on an open fire. He had cooked on the ranches of West Texas during roundups for the past 65 years and was a master with a Dutch oven and hot coals.

I discovered early on that one of the smartest things I could do was to make good friends with the cook. We were awakened each morning at four o'clock to the smell of hot coffee, fresh biscuits, and fried bacon.

We cowboys slept in bedrolls around the blazing campfire. There was always a race for the coffeepot first thing. The key was to get it while it was fresh because the coffee grounds always settled to the bottom. No one wanted to get stuck with the last cup.

Ramón couldn't help but notice that I was eating alone that morning at breakfast, shunned by the other cowboys. He offered me a little advice. "Whatever you do this morning, make sure when you come down the mountain for lunch that you have some cattle with you. You have to prove you can pull your own weight." He went on to explain how the cattle in this part of the country were wild, and many of them had never seen a horse, much less a man. He told me they would have a tendency to run the other way and bunch up in the brush.

> Character is higher than intellect.
> A great soul will be strong to live as well as think.
>
> RALPH WALDO EMERSON

The foreman sent the five of us in separate directions that morning to begin the roundup. I felt like I didn't have a friend in the world. It's not too hard to get lost on 25,000 acres, especially if you've never been there before. But I accepted the challenge and rode off as if I were an experienced hand. After about an hour's ride, I heard some cattle over a distant hilltop and moved in their direction. Ramón's advice was right. The cows saw me before I saw them and ran toward a high plateau. I knew I had my work cut out for me.

I must have run back and forth for miles before I managed to gather a young bull, 18 mothers, and 5 calves. You can believe I was counting them. Ramón's words had made a deep impression. Finally I pushed them down the rocky terrain toward camp. There was always one that didn't want to follow the rest of the herd and was continually breaking out for the opposite direction. On several occasions, big mule deer that were lying in the deep grass would suddenly jump up and spook the whole bunch, forcing me to start almost from scratch.

A morning alone on horseback in the middle of nowhere allows a lot of time for thought. I began to contemplate the importance of discipline. I was slightly more than agitated at my situation. I could have let the one cow go, but I realized at this point that diligence and self-control must prevail. I was responsible for the cows and intended to do my job to the best of my ability. I was reminded of one of my favorite passages from Scripture:

> For this very reason, make every effort to add to your faith goodness; and to goodness, knowledge; and to knowledge, self-control; and to self-control, perseverance; and to perseverance, godliness; and to godliness, mutual affection; and to mutual affection, love. For if you possess these qualities in increasing measure, they will keep you from being ineffective and unproductive in your knowledge of our Lord Jesus Christ. But whoever does not have them is nearsighted and blind, forgetting that they have been cleansed from their past sins (2 Peter 1:5-9).

If ever I needed this passage, it was now. When I topped the last hill and saw the chuck wagon, I realized I was late for the dinner bell. I penned the cattle I'd found. I could see from a distance the smile on Ramón's face as he pointed in my direction. I noticed all eyes were turned toward me. When I sauntered over to get lunch, I tried to hide my stiffness from the long ride. To tell the truth, I was hurting from head to toe. I wasn't accustomed to that much riding, especially in mountainous terrain. Fortunately for my ego, the cowboys overlooked my obvious discomfort with congratulations and slaps on the back for a job well done. They offered me a seat by the fire, a full plate of lunch, and lively conversation. I was now one of the boys.

In life, a person's reputation is formed by the opinion of others. It is the foundation on which trust and respect are built. We can't determine what other people will think of us; we can only determine what they ought to think about us. Strong character is developed when we are faithful to do the right thing no matter how insignificant and inconsequential it may seem at the time.

3

Success: Living His Dream

My grandfather was a man who knew where he was going and why. He was able to see clearly even through the fog and mist of hardship and suffering. He was a man of strong convictions and he was always optimistic about the future. When I was just a young child, I thought he was the smartest man who had ever lived and wondered how such a successful man could be so gentle and kind. Granddaddy Mason shared his secret with me, and it has been my favorite Bible verse for as long as I can remember: "Keep this Book of the Law always on your lips; meditate on it day and night, so that you may be careful to do everything written in it. Then you will be prosperous and successful" (Joshua 1:8).

The world today measures success in how much wealth we can acquire. The rich and famous are often placed on pedestals and admired by millions for their accomplishments. I tend to agree with Albert Einstein when he said, "A successful man is he who receives a great deal from his fellowmen, usually incomparably more than corresponds to his service to them. The value of a man, however, should be seen in what he gives and not in what he is able to receive."

True success in life is determined by how well we handle the seemingly "little things" in relation to the things we view as most important. In 1928, just prior to the Great Depression, Granddaddy was prospering in the cattle and sheep business. With five children and another on the way, he decided it was time my grandmother learned how to drive a car. Few women from the surrounding ranches could drive. The men generally went into town and took care of the shopping while the women spent their days taking care of the family chores. Granddaddy thought the old Model T Ford would be too difficult for Mamaw, so one day he drove home in a new green Chevrolet. It was a fancy, four-door family car that had gear shifts and even windows that rolled up and down. He was especially proud of that because when it rained they had to always stop to put the curtains up on the Model T. They were now a two-car family.

> Success is the sum of small efforts—repeated day in and day out.
>
> ROBERT COLLIER

Mamaw had always been handy with a mule team and wagon, and she took to driving her new car in short order with Granddaddy's instruction. They drove all over the ranch as he patiently told her every move to make until she was ready to solo. It wasn't long before she was driving into town to shop for family and friends. While few people owned even one car, they had two. The neighbors in the community viewed them as very successful.

I think the greatest success, however, was that a devoted husband realized the value of a wife and mother who had sacrificed everything for years to care for the ones she loved. She had worked the fields, driven the wagons, raised her own poultry and vegetables, made her own soap, washed the clothes by hand, and always had three hot meals on the table that she prepared from her wood stove. He chose to honor her with a new car. That was Granddaddy's way of saying, "You are a very valuable woman and a very successful wife and mother." Proverbs 31:26-29 describes Mamaw well: "She speaks with wisdom, and faithful instruction is on her tongue. She watches over the affairs of her household and does not eat the bread of idleness. Her children arise and call her blessed; her husband also, and he praises her: 'Many women do noble things, but you surpass them all.'"

What have I taken to heart from my grandparents' lives? I traveled down two different trails in my pursuit of success. One was *my* way. It left me disappointed, dejected, unfulfilled, and alone. I thought it wasn't necessary to follow the guidance of my family; I could make it on my own. With no place left to turn, I decided to try God's trail and discovered His Word is true. Hebrews 6:12 best explains the important heritage my family has left me: "We do not want you to become lazy, but to imitate those who through faith and patience inherit what has been promised."

In your own search for success, I urge you to hear these words:

> Blessed is the one who does not walk in step with the wicked or stand in the way that sinners take or sit in the company of mockers, but whose delight is in the law of the LORD, and who meditates on his law day and night. That person is like a tree planted by streams of water, which yields its fruit in season and whose leaf does not wither—whatever they do prospers (Psalm 1:1-3).

Adversity:
If It Weren't for Bad Luck...

As a young teenager, my grandfather worked as a cowboy on a cattle drive from the King Ranch in South Texas to the railhead in Abilene, Kansas. It was a long and sometimes difficult journey. The weather was often severe, demanding the cowboy's expert attention at all times.

As the herd approached the vast plains of West Texas, a ferocious thunderstorm roared in the blustering skies above. With less than half the journey completed, the first obstacle of the drive occurred. The cattle became increasingly nervous, spooked by the powerful wind and crackling lightning. The once tightly held herd began to scatter, moving outwardly toward the cowboys riding swing and flank. The experienced hands knew the cattle were likely to stampede, and it was their task to keep them calm and in a tight bunch along the trail.

As the lead steers nervously approached a grassy hilltop, they startled an immense herd of buffalo that had migrated south in search of sustaining grasslands. Much to the dismay of the cowboys, the cattle caught sight of the buffalo and a stampede was now unavoidable.

Lightning exploded above them as the ground thundered below the powerful hoofbeats of the two herds. They ran over three miles that disastrous afternoon. The chuck wagon and supplies were destroyed in the valley below. The remuda of saddle horses was scattered for miles around, and some were never recovered.

The storm blew over about sundown, and the trail boss gathered his men around the campfire and made plans for the roundup. The cowboys were exhausted, but they chased those cows for more than eight miles before containing the herd. Some galloped off into the darkness to recover the remaining cattle and horses. The men returned at sunrise with all but a few missing strays. Both the cowboys and the cattle were rewarded with a day's rest before returning to the Kansas trail.

Just as Granddad was caught in the perils of the stampede, we too find that life has its stormy and sometimes disastrous side. Storms come in many forms—tornadoes, earthquakes, floods, illnesses, accidents, angry

words—and they all cause seemingly irreparable damage to our lives. If God is truly in control of the storms in the skies, He is also in control of the storms in our lives. Moses wrote, "When you are in distress and all these things have happened to you, then in later days you will return to the LORD your God and obey him" (Deuteronomy 4:30).

So often storms of distraction sweep through our lives and blow us completely off the trail to our destination. Just as the cowboy keeps an eye on the weather and an ear to the ground, we too must be attentive to the storms around us and listen to the voice of God. We must realize that the storm is a friendly reminder that we are drifting from the trail the Lord has set before us. Psalm 34:17 says, "The righteous cry out, and the LORD hears them; he delivers them from all their troubles."

Unfortunately, life is not always easy. Adversity will most definitely come our way. When it does, think of the cowboys like my grandfather and his friends on the trail who thought, "If it weren't for bad luck…" and remember that when the storm is over, there is a place of rest and a voice that will guide you safely back onto the trail. Jesus promises, "Come to me, all you who are weary and burdened, and I will give you rest. Take my yoke upon you and learn from me, for I am gentle and humble in heart, and you will find rest for your souls. For my yoke is easy and my burden is light" (Matthew 11:28-30).

Contentment: End of a Long Day

American cowboys may be the world's foremost experts on contentment. It seems to be an unwritten code they live by. The Maker of the universe has destined them to be caretakers of the land and the livestock. It doesn't matter if the sun is shining, the snow is falling, or the wind is howling—the cowboys have a job to do. They always find something positive no matter how inconvenient the situation. Everything seems to work together for the good in the overall scheme of things. Romans 8:28 says, "We know that in all things God works for the good of those who love him, who have been called according to his purpose." The cowboy knows his calling and his purpose. He never complains about the rain; he knows it is necessary to produce the grass that sustains his livestock. A contented mind is the greatest blessing a person can enjoy in this world.

While rounding up cattle on a large West Texas ranch late one fall afternoon, I watched an interesting scene transpire. The sun was setting in the west, and the large herd of cattle that had moved on ahead filled the sky with dust, causing a haze over the Davis Mountains in the background. A job that began around the campfire at four in the morning would soon be complete. As a cowboy riding a white horse sat tall in the saddle to take in the magnificent view, the last few head of stragglers were pushed into the corral below.

It would be easy to complain about the exploits of the day's cattle drive. We had driven, roped, vaccinated, and branded more than 250 cows. It had been hot and dusty. We'd been kicked and stepped on. We'd breathed in dust and the acrid smoke from burning cowhide.

Now we were tired and hungry, but never once did I hear anyone complain. I was suddenly reminded of what the apostle Paul wrote:

> I have learned to be content whatever the circumstances. I know what it is to be in need, and I know what it is to have plenty. I have learned the secret of being content in any and every situation, whether well fed or hungry, whether living in plenty or in want. I can do all this through him who gives me strength (Philippians 4:11-13).

The cowboy knows his purpose in life and is content to gladly do his job, no matter what the circumstances may be. Far from the ranchlands of West Texas, however, discontentment surrounds most of our lives. Our lack of contentment stems from a notion that we have to have the newest, the biggest, and the best of everything. Advertisers attempt to convince everyone that we are either too fat or we are too skinny or our automobiles aren't classy or sporty enough to convince others of our success. We complain when it rains and when it doesn't. It is usually too hot or too cold. It seems few are content with who they are, what they look like, and what they have.

The primary reason so few find contentment is due to the pursuit of money and self-gratification. The writer of the book of Hebrews wrote:

> Keep your lives free from the love of money and be content with what you have, because God has said, "Never will I leave you; never will I forsake you." So we say with confidence, "The Lord is my helper; I will not be afraid. What can mere mortals do to me?" Remember your leaders, who spoke the word of God to you. Consider the outcome of their way of life and imitate their faith. Jesus Christ is the same yesterday and today and forever (Hebrews 13:5-8).

The cowboy has learned to depend on God, trusting that He will supply everything he needs to sustain his way of life. When our goal is the pursuit of material things, we are ignoring God's promise to supply all we need. We need to be content with what we have, but never be satisfied in our pursuit of excellence in Him.

6

Courage:
The Riders of Mystic Canyon

arly in my career as an artist, I was invited to the small West Texas border town of Lajitas to do an art exhibit at a local museum. Lajitas was once a trading post that was used for more than 200 years by traders from Spain, Mexico, and Texas. The current owner of the trading post at the time of my exhibit was a colorful character who had many tales and stories passed down from his great-grandfather, the founder of the post. This area has a rich culture, and the natives are a very superstitious people.

During my visit I met a young man named Juan. He was from Mexico and had crossed the Rio Grande seeking a prosperous future in America. When he found out I was an artist, he thought I might have some interest in painting what he described as one of the most beautiful places in all of Mexico. Directly south of Lajitas is a vast and often treacherous desert. The small village he called home was some 80 miles away. He eagerly offered to guide me there to photograph the scenery and meet his family.

Early the next morning, Juan's brother met us across the border in his pickup, and we began our long and dusty journey. The truck broke down on two occasions, but we managed to enter the small village by noon that hot summer day. We were cordially greeted by his mother. Although she spoke no English, I felt welcomed by her warmth and hospitality and enjoyed a traditional Mexican lunch of stacked enchiladas that she'd prepared in my honor.

Juan's brother left after lunch and soon joined us with three horses. We promptly began our journey to the canyon. Juan related many of the superstitions about the mysterious locale as we rode through the Mexican desert. Natives in the area believed it to be haunted. There were century-old tales of people who entered the canyon never to be seen again. It was believed that after the sun had set in the west, various ghosts and apparitions could be heard moving throughout the canyon walls.

When we arrived at our destination, the first thing I saw was a crystal clear stream of water pouring from massive rocks leading into the canyon. I thought this to be most unusual as I had not seen water since we crossed the Rio Grande, some 80 miles to the north. I asked Juan if he thought it was safe to ride down into the canyon, admitting some anxiousness on my part. Soon the sun would set, magnifying my apprehension. It was here I remembered a Bible verse about water flowing out from between the rocks. David described it as part of the wanderings of the children of Israel: "He split the rocks in the wilderness and gave them water as abundant as the seas; he brought streams out of a rocky crag and made water flow down like rivers" (Psalm 78:15-16). I imagined this area to be identical to that as we entered the canyon between the massive rock bluffs on either side.

> Courage is being scared to death—and saddling up anyway.
>
> JOHN WAYNE

The temperature outside the canyon was more than 100 degrees, but as soon as we entered the canyon, it dropped dramatically. Waterfalls flowed directly from holes in the large crevices above our heads. Ferns and other vegetation grew everywhere, as though we were in a tropical forest. Not a word was spoken as we slowly guided our horses down the narrow path leading to a 50-foot waterfall at the back of the canyon.

As the path ended, we were forced to turn a corner. Juan pointed to a rock outcropping where pictographs had been painted by ancient ones hundreds of years ago. As I stopped to examine the images, the wind blew eerily between the canyon walls. I never thought I was superstitious until I looked at the sky and suddenly became aware of the impending darkness. I was in a foreign country with strangers, and no one knew of my whereabouts. The shrill howling of coyotes filled the night air. I was overwhelmed with uncertainty and anxious to return to safety. We made our way back, and I was truly elated to see the smile on the face of Juan's mother when we arrived at her home that evening.

There are many occasions in life where we are in unfamiliar situations that require us to have courage. We need to have the mental and moral strength to persevere and withstand danger, fear, and difficulty. We need to heed the words God spoke to Joshua:

> Be strong and very courageous. Be careful to obey all the law my servant Moses gave you; do not turn from it to the right or to the left, that you may be successful wherever you go. Keep this Book of the Law always on your lips; meditate on it day and night, so that you may be careful to do everything written in it. Then you will be prosperous and successful. Have I not commanded you? Be strong and courageous. Do not be afraid; do not be discouraged, for the LORD your God will be with you wherever you go (Joshua 1:7-9).

Family:
When Della Rode with Daddy

The year was 1929, and my grandparents and other members of the family were living on a ranch near Eden, Texas. Families were generally large in those days because it took many hands to manage the ranch chores in the most economical manner. This was the first year of the Great Depression, and many people were having a difficult time making their land payments and maintaining their properties. Quite a few people had no place to live and little food to eat. There were five children in the Mason household at that time, plus grandparents and a number of aunts and uncles. My grandfather was an astute rancher and businessman who managed to survive comfortably during these hard times. It was not unusual for him to reach out to assist friends and neighbors who were in financial need.

My mother was born that year, the last of six children. My grandmother, an amazing woman, delivered all her babies at home. No doctor was available at the time, but living in ranch country, they had a veterinarian friend who assisted with the delivery. My mother grew to be the apple of her father's eye. She always loved riding horseback with her dad while tending to various ranch chores. Most of the other children were considerably older and had their own responsibilities around the ranch. She cherished the time she spent with her dad.

My mother was three years old and enjoyed every minute riding Old Dan with her dad. It was that year Granddad bought her a black Shetland pony. Her name was Patsy, and Mother rode her almost every day. She was too young to ride the distance from pasture to pasture, so oftentimes Granddaddy would take the backseat out of the old

Model T Ford, load Patsy in the back, and drive Mother to the next pasture so she could ride out with the cowhands.

Love and dedication bound their large family together. Everyone was important and valued, each contributing to the well-being of the others. They understood the importance of working together, taking to heart the passage from Ecclesiastes that says:

> Two are better than one, because they have a good return for their labor: If either of them falls down, one can help the other up. But pity anyone who falls and has no one to help them up. Also, if two lie down together, they will keep warm. But how can one keep warm alone? Though one may be overpowered, two can defend themselves. A cord of three strands is not quickly broken (Ecclesiastes 4:9-12).

Granddaddy Mason lived his life by God's principles and passed them down to his family. He always modeled the characteristics of godliness. He exemplified the fruit of the Spirit, which is "love, joy, peace, forbearance, kindness, goodness, faithfulness, gentleness and self-control" (Galatians 5:22-23).

The United States was established as one nation under God, yet we as a society have drifted farther and farther away from the principles that directed our founding fathers and guided our families. Biblical principles are the backbone of our Constitution and have guided families for generations, yet society continues to move away from these values. From the once agriculturally based economy to the Industrial Revolution, and presently into the age of high technology, priorities have changed. Family members who once lived and worked together as a unit are today independent and often separated by many miles, each one pursuing his or her own goals and aspirations.

When we take time to reflect on lifestyles and priorities of the past century, we must surely notice that we have drifted from the principles that were so important to our families. Perhaps the words of David can steer us back on the right trail:

> Unless the LORD builds the house, the builders labor in vain. Unless the LORD watches over the city, the guards stand watch in vain. In vain you rise early and stay up late, toiling for food to eat—for he grants sleep to those he loves (Psalm 127:1-2).

SHARE WITH BERNIE

Faith:
Morning on the Merced

aving been born and raised in Texas, I had never experienced anything like Yosemite National Park in California. As I drove the winding roads leading into the park to meet a friend, I will never forget the impression I had on viewing the Yosemite Valley for the first time. I was so overwhelmed by the landscape I couldn't drive farther. I stopped the car and got out, lost in the magnitude of God's glorious creation. I felt so insignificant in comparison to its grandeur.

Eventually I continued my journey down the mountain, and was overcome again by the mammoth size of the sequoia trees guarding the entrance into the park. Yosemite National Park includes nearly 1200 square miles of the most breathtaking scenery in the world.

Upon arriving at my friend's cabin, I was happy to find that he had prepared mountain horses for our journey along various wilderness trails. As eagles soared in the skies above us, we rode to vistas where the view seemed to stretch an eternity away. The mountain paths took us past roaring waterfalls cascading hundreds of feet down towering walls of shining granite. As we continued past rushing mountain streams and calm jade lakes to an alpine meadow, I was consumed by the presence of the Lord.

I was reminded of Psalm 46:10: "Be still, and know that I am God; I will be exalted among the nations, I will be exalted in the earth." When we stand quietly before the Lord and honor Him with our reverence and praise Him for His power and majesty, He is faithful to reward us with His presence.

Faith is a precious gift from God. The writer of Hebrews tells us:

Faith is confidence in what we hope for and assurance about what we do not see. This is what the ancients were commended for. By faith we understand that the universe was formed at God's command, so that what is seen was not made of what was visible (Hebrews 11:1).

Faith is something that is sure and certain. Faith begins when we believe that God is who He says He is. When we take God at His word and believe His promises, then we are demonstrating true faith.

If you want to experience a faith-building relationship with the Creator of the universe, Jesus said, "Ask and it will be given to you; seek and you will find; knock and the door will be opened to you. For everyone who asks receives; the one who seeks finds; and to the one who knocks, the door will be opened" (Matthew 7:7-8).

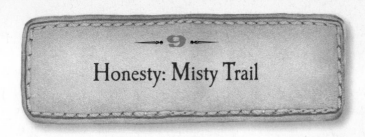

Honesty: Misty Trail

owboys often contended with some type of adversity in their daily routines. Foggy mornings can be especially difficult when searching for stray cattle. There have been many occasions where I have rounded up cattle and pushed them to the corrals to get a head count, only to realize there were still strays left behind in the fog. Sometimes shadows and images hidden by the fog are not at all what they appear to be when we get a closer look. Fog can be very deceiving.

Unfortunately, life is often foggy due to deception and dishonesty. Honesty is one of the most valuable qualities anyone can possess. It is the foundation of all that is high in character among people. The world is always looking for honest men and women, for people who can be trusted and who will fight for the truth without compromise. People who will look us in the eye and tell us the truth. Men and women who are not too lazy to work and not too proud to be poor. Men and women whose word is their bond. We need to be careful not to be deceived into thinking we can compromise truth just because we've seen so many others prosper in dishonesty with no apparent or obvious consequences. Remember the boy who cried wolf?

My grandfather was known throughout Texas as an honest man. Most of his business transactions were closed with a handshake because his word was as good as gold. During the Depression years, the cattle market plummeted. Many Texas ranchers found themselves unable to pay their debts, and many banks foreclosed on ranches. Granddaddy knew that many of his neighbors were in jeopardy of losing their homes and livelihoods.

Being the man of character that he was, he reached out with a helping hand. There wasn't much of a market for cattle at the time, but Granddaddy knew that the King Ranch in South Texas was buying cattle for 50 cents a head. He contacted his needy neighbors and arranged to combine their cattle with his and drive them to the King Ranch for sale. He promised prompt payment for their livestock. He had no contracts, attorneys, or promissory notes.

> I am one of those who would rather sink with faith than swim without it.
>
> STANLEY BALDWIN

Granddaddy assembled a few friends, gathered all of the cattle, and began the 500-mile journey to the King Ranch. I remember his description of the destitution of many people along the trail. He ran across families who had lost everything in the Depression and were camping with their children along the roadside. They had very little to eat, and their eyes were filled with hopelessness.

The herd arrived intact at the King Ranch several weeks later. The cattle were penned and tallied. Granddaddy was paid 50 cents per animal, a paltry sum by common standards, but a much-needed blessing nevertheless.

His companions on the trail drive shared stories upon their return of how Granddaddy had generously shared money, provisions, and food with many of the poverty-stricken families along the trail. It was told that he was always careful to give away only his share, never compromising the money due his neighbors for their cattle.

When I read Matthew 5:14-16, I think of my grandfather's honest and unwavering character:

> You are the light of the world. A town built on a hill cannot be hidden. Neither do people light a lamp and put it under a bowl. Instead they put it on its stand, and it gives light to everyone in the house. In the same way, let your light shine before others, that they may see your good deeds and glorify your Father in heaven.

My grandfather was a perfect example of what we all should strive to be.

10
Forgiveness: Pays the Same, Rain or Shine

SHARE WITH PETER

Everyone makes mistakes. One of the hardest things for most of us to extend is forgiveness. We are quick to blame, judge, and criticize others. But Jesus said:

> Why do you look at the speck of sawdust in your brother's eye and pay no attention to the plank in your own eye? How can you say to your brother, "Let me take the speck out of your eye," when all the time there is a plank in your own eye? You hypocrite, first take the plank out of your own eye, and then you will see clearly to remove the speck from your brother's eye (Matthew 7:3-5).

This is simple advice, but it seems to be one of the most difficult principles to practice!

One rainy autumn day marked the beginning of the fall cow works. We were riding from the ranch headquarters to a distant pasture to set up camp around the chuck wagon for a weeklong stay. One of the most miserable things for a cowboy is a long ride in a wet saddle. Since cowboys never complain about the rain, they knew it was time to don their slickers and mount up when ranch foreman Jim met them that morning at the tack room and said, "Well, boys, we pay the same, rain or shine."

And a long day it was, indeed. The rain fell relentlessly for hours, making for a difficult trip through the mountainous terrain. The ground was muddy and slick—especially for the mules pulling the heavily loaded chuck wagon. They had great difficulty negotiating the steep inclines, often sliding out of control. Upon nearing their destination, it was necessary to descend the mountainous plateau before reaching the campsite in the meadow below.

The wagon boss had a tight grip on the reins as the mules cautiously approached the edge of the plateau and began to make their way down the mountain. He failed to notice the clear path to the right and instead headed directly for the rocks. At that very moment, the weight of the wagon was too much for the mules to control, and it began to slide down the rocky slope. A wheel caught on a large rock outcropping, forcing the wagon onto its side. It threw both men from the wagon, but somehow the mules stayed on their feet. Spooked as they were by the crash, they ran for the meadow below, dragging the wagon behind them. The provisions were scattered all the way down the muddy hillside.

Fortunately no one was injured during this disastrous beginning. After the rain stopped, the men were able to tie their lariats onto the wagon and, using the strength of their horses, they pulled it upright and gathered the provisions from the mountainside. The camp was finally set up, a fire was built, and the cowboys were able to relax with cups of coffee.

It would have been very easy for the men to blame the wagon boss for his mistake, but instead all was forgiven. "It could have happened to anybody. Don't worry about it. I'm just glad no one was hurt," said Jim.

Everyone makes mistakes. Some appear to be more serious than others, but in God's eyes, our responsibility is the same. We must forgive everything. Jesus said, "If you forgive other people when they sin against you, your heavenly Father will also forgive you. But if you do not forgive others their sins, your Father will not forgive your sins" (Matthew 6:14-15). He also said, "Be merciful, just as your Father is merciful. Do not judge, and you will not be judged. Do not condemn, and you will not be condemned. Forgive, and you will be forgiven" (Luke 6:36-37).

> Friendships flourish at the fountain of forgiveness.
>
> WILLIAM ARTHUR WARD

Love: Crossing the Nueces

The Nueces River is one of the most beautiful sights in Texas. Artesian springs supply crystal-clear water that flows for many miles over a limestone rock bottom through the hill country. I'd been gathering a herd of longhorn cattle with friends, and we found ourselves working much later than we had intended that day. A full moon was rising in the east. What a spectacular sight it was, with its white light glistening on the surrounding hills and trees and reflecting from the splashing water under the cattle's hooves.

I recall gazing down into the river as I rode across, thinking how muddy and disturbed the usually clear and calm water was. After crossing the river and penning the longhorns, I walked back down to the shoreline and sat on the bank. I was mesmerized by the intensity of the moon illuminating the Lord's creation surrounding me. I gazed into the water, which was now calm and returning to its normal clarity.

Life is oftentimes like that river. Things may appear clear one minute and muddy the next. When we stray from the foundational principles the Lord has set before us, the waters of life become choppy and muddy. But as we return to God's principles of faith, hope, and love, the waters will gradually become clear and calm again.

I believe love is the greatest of all human qualities because God is love and His love is the source of our love. The most thorough explanation of love is found in the Bible:

> If I have the gift of prophecy and can fathom all mysteries and all knowledge, and if I have a faith that can move mountains, but do not have love, I am nothing. If I give all I possess to the poor and give over my body to hardship that I may boast, but do not have love, I gain nothing.

Love is patient, love is kind. It does not envy, it does not boast, it is not proud. It does not dishonor others, it is not self-seeking, it is not easily angered, it keeps no record of wrongs. Love does not delight in evil but rejoices with the truth. It always protects, always trusts, always hopes, always perseveres.

Love never fails. But where there are prophecies, they will cease; where there are tongues, they will be stilled; where there is knowledge, it will pass away. For we know in part and we prophesy in part, but when completeness comes, what is in part disappears.

When I was a child, I talked like a child, I thought like a child, I reasoned like a child. When I became a man, I put the ways of childhood behind me. For now we see only a reflection as in a mirror; then we shall see face to face. Now I know in part; then I shall know fully, even as I am fully known.

And now these three remain: faith, hope and love. But the greatest of these is love (1 Corinthians 13:2-12).

Without love it is impossible to be truly productive or effective in any aspect of life, whether it be our personal relationships, our professions, or our spiritual service. The Bible teaches that love is unconditional and must be directed outward toward others rather than inward toward ourselves. We are instructed to give, expecting nothing in return, and to love others more than we love ourselves. This kind of love contradicts our natural inclinations toward self-centeredness. I am slowly beginning to understand the only way to attain this love for others is to ensure that my faith, which is founded on God's Word, and my hope, which is a joyful expectation of eternal salvation, are in proper perspective.

It is almost impossible to imagine what this world would be like if we all adhered to the words of the apostle Paul: "Do nothing out of selfish ambition or vain conceit. Rather, in humility value others above yourselves" (Philippians 2:3). This is God's plan, and therein lies our map for the trail before us.

Wisdom: The Last Bunch

When I was three years old, I sat at the knee of my grandmother and watched her paint beautiful landscapes and still lifes. At that early age, I had a strong desire to draw and imitate what she was doing. My family realized I had a special gift and was very encouraging and supportive. As the years passed, I sought instruction and counsel from successful professionals. I knew by the age of 12 that God had a plan for my life.

I've discovered it's critical to seek wisdom in order to discover what plan God has for each of our lives. The writer of Proverbs said, "In their hearts humans plan their course, but the LORD establishes their steps" (Proverbs 16:9). So many times in life we think we have enough wisdom so we don't need advice from anyone, but it's easy to evaluate our wisdom—or the lack of it—by the way we act and the decisions we make. I've made many wrong decisions in my life and have suffered the consequences. I'm certain that had I sought godly wisdom and righteous counsel, most of those wrong decisions could have been avoided.

The book of Proverbs defines wisdom in a few simple verses: "The fear of the LORD is the beginning of wisdom, and knowledge of the Holy One is understanding" (9:10). "The way of fools seems right to them, but the wise listen to advice" (12:15). "Plans fail for lack of counsel, but with many advisers they succeed" (15:22).

We all make many decisions in our lives, and it is imperative that we seek God's guidance and wisdom in even the smallest matters. Sometimes His answers come immediately, and sometimes they take much longer. On those occasions, it is best to have patience, just as Abraham did. God said to Abraham, "I will surely bless you and give you many descendants." Then, "after waiting patiently, Abraham received what was promised" (Hebrews 6:14-15). Abraham waited 25 years for the fulfillment of the son God promised him.

God *always* keeps His promises. When we feel like we have waited an eternity for an answer or direction, the Bible and the counsel of mature Christians encourage us to wait for God to meet our needs in His perfect timing.

My grandfather shared the wisdom necessary for being a successful rancher with his family. He passed down the importance of being a good husband and father. He taught us how to be a good steward of the land and how to care for livestock. Things we can't learn in school, such as stretching a fence straight and true or throwing a rope with precision, are best mastered at the hand of an experienced professional.

> The trail is the thing, not the end of the trail. Travel too fast and you miss all you are traveling for.
>
> LOUIS L'AMOUR

Wisdom can be absorbed from the wise like a sponge absorbs water—if we are willing to heed the opportunity. God's plans for us are full of opportunities! He is a rewarder of those who diligently seek Him. The apostle Paul wrote, "We know that in all things God works for the good of those who love him, who have been called according to his purpose" (Romans 8:28).

The wise writer of Proverbs said it this way:

> Listen, my sons, to a father's instruction; pay attention and gain understanding. I give you sound learning, so do not forsake my teaching. For I too was a son to my father, still tender, and cherished by my mother. Then he taught me, and he said to me, "Take hold of my words with all your heart; keep my commands, and you will live. Get wisdom, get understanding; do not forget my words or turn away from them. Do not forsake wisdom, and she will protect you; love her, and she will watch over you.

"The beginning of wisdom is this: Get wisdom. Though it cost all you have, get understanding. Cherish her, and she will exalt you; embrace her, and she will honor you. She will give you a garland to grace your head and present you with a glorious crown."

Listen, my son, accept what I say, and the years of your life will be many. I instruct you in the way of wisdom and lead you along straight paths. When you walk, your steps will not be hampered; when you run, you will not stumble. Hold on to instruction, do not let it go; guard it well, for it is your life (Proverbs 4:1-13).

Prayer: The Chase

I was driving through New Mexico late one summer afternoon as a rain shower was passing in front of the setting sun. I noticed a lone cowboy in the distance with his rope in the wind while in hot pursuit of a wild mustang. Over the next few minutes I watched him throw his rope unsuccessfully as the dust rose above the flowering yellow chamissa blooms. He was determined to catch that horse despite the roar of lightning in the background and the threat of imminent rain. After several tries, he finally captured the mustang and led him across the vast prairie. His persistence had paid off.

When I think of prayer and my own prayer life, the image of that cowboy comes to mind. Am I persistent in prayer? Sometimes it seems that God answers our prayers quickly, and other times it seems like He may never answer us at all. But Scripture promises, "This is the confidence we have in approaching God: that if we ask anything according to his will, he hears us. And if we know that he hears—whatever we ask—we know that we have what we asked of him" (1 John 5:14-15). The answer to our prayers will either be "yes," "no," or "wait." God has a plan for each of our lives, and He answers our prayers according to His will and in His timing. Oftentimes it requires persistence on our part as we strive to improve our ability to hear Him. Like the cowboy chasing the mustang, we must keep praying through the distractions of life.

My friends Bryan and Kristen Winfield discovered the power of persistence in their prayer life. They wanted to have children for a long time, but a medical problem convinced their doctors it would never be possible. But through prayer, my friends experienced God-given hope and their faith remained strong. They prayed earnestly for five years—both privately and within their church family. They sensed God was telling them He was in control of the situation and that they should wait patiently.

Kristen conceived the week of Easter, and their faith and prayers were rewarded with the birth of a son the week before Christmas, much to the amazement of the doctors. God had answered their prayers with a healthy and handsome baby boy to perpetuate their family name.

My grandmother prayed for her family's salvation for many years before God answered her prayers. Most of the old-time cowboys were uncomfortable in church and would seldom attend. They weren't accustomed to the confinement they felt inside the four walls and were much more comfortable appreciating the Lord's creation on the back of a trusty horse. My granddad was no exception.

Grandmother was faithful and determined. She persisted for years. She attended church regularly and frequented the many revivals that came through the small West Texas ranching communities. God answered her prayers one summer during a revival. She convinced Granddad to go with her one night, and, much to his surprise, he found the preacher to be "a real likable fellow." The two of them struck up a friendship, and he was baptized that very week and remained a strong and diligent church member for the remainder of his life. The change in him affected all six children and brought stability and purpose to the family. The power and persistence of the prayers of one woman changed the lives of an entire family forever. She was living proof of James 5:16: "The prayer of a righteous person is powerful and effective."

Over the years I've witnessed many answered prayers. Some have been miraculous physical healings, while others have been guidance through difficult times. But hearing that still small voice, that nudge or impression that comes so faithfully from God when I need it the most, is my greatest joy. I encourage you to "pray continually" (1 Thessalonians 5:17).

14

Humility:
Summer Shadows

Granddad was truly a man of honor and humility. He remains one of the greatest influences in my life. He used to enjoy leisurely rides through the countryside. When we rode together, he would talk about nature and explain how perfectly designed God's creation is. He often commented on how insignificant he felt by comparison. It was during these valuable times that I learned the true meaning of humility.

Granddad took his job as cowboy and cattleman seriously. He understood his responsibility as a steward of the land and livestock. His many years as a cowboy had taught him the necessity of following the natural order God had designed to be successful as a rancher and in life. He was a humble servant who did his best to care for the portion of creation God had entrusted him with.

This attitude was also reflected in his family life. He was the father of six children and cared for many other family members, including his parents and my grandmother's parents in their later years. He often cared for his brother and sister as well. Life proved difficult at times, especially for ranching families who depended on a good economy and favorable weather conditions. Events like the Depression and the Dust Bowl drought devastated many families. I recall asking him when I was a child why he took care of so many people. His simple reply was straight out of Romans 14:12: "'Each of us will give an account of ourselves to God.' And I want to have a clean slate." Granddad remained a humble servant, always sharing unselfishly with his entire family, paying careful attention to their health and well-being.

Whenever friends and neighbors had a need, Granddad would be the first to lend a helping hand. Many people lost everything they had during the Depression, and on many occasions Granddad provided food, clothing, and money to help sustain those families. He wasn't a wealthy man, just a hardworking, humble servant who discovered that as he helped others, God was always faithful to meet his needs. Jesus said, "Give to everyone who asks you, and if anyone takes what belongs to you, do not demand it back. Do to others as you would have them do to you" (Luke 6:30-31). He went on to promise, "Give, and it will be given to you. A good measure, pressed down, shaken together and running over, will be poured into your lap. For with the measure you use, it will be measured to you" (verse 38).

Granddad loved to talk of the wonders of God's great creation. The beauty of a sunrise and the birth of a new calf were among his great delights. He found pleasure sitting in a pasture of deep grass studying a herd of cattle while chewing on a piece of straw. He taught me many things on our rides, most of which I haven't really understood until now. You see, he never said the word "humility." He just lived it.

Granddad has been with the Lord many years now, enjoying the rewards of being a faithful servant. But the image of that wonderful man is planted firmly in my mind. That great American cowboy stood tall and proud—his white shirt buttoned at the top, one pant leg draped gracefully over the top of his finely stitched riding boots, and his cattleman Stetson cocked slightly to the side.

Humility like darkness reveals the heavenly lights.

HENRY DAVID THOREAU

I will never forget the smile he always wore and the good word he had for everyone. A true "gentle" man he was.

It is my privilege to step into his place. I have been blessed with three wonderful grandsons: Hunter, Jordan, and Andrew, and two precious granddaughters, Haley and Abby. It is incumbent upon me to share the life of this great man with them and everyone else. His humility and fear of the Lord brought him honor and a long life. God's desire is for that to be perpetuated for all generations.

The challenge before each of us is to "live it" as my granddad did. When we lay aside selfishness and look to the interest of others, we become more like Christ, the perfect example of humility. Our goal is to be that of humble servants. These words from the apostle Paul are the key to order and honor in our lives. They are our guide on this great trail ride:

> Make my joy complete by being like-minded, having the same love, being one in spirit and of one mind. Do nothing out of selfish ambition or vain conceit. Rather, in humility value others above yourselves, not looking to your own interests but each of you to the interests of others. In your relationships with one another, have the same mindset as Christ Jesus (Philippians 2:2-5).

Part 2

PRAYERS ALONG THE TRAIL

15

Our Father in Heaven

So many books have been written on the subject of prayer throughout the years because it is such a tremendous blessing to be able to communicate directly with the Creator of all things. This great privilege belongs to everyone who invites Jesus Christ to come live within their heart. God has provided a way of salvation through the sacrifice of His Son for everyone who will believe.

In this section we're going to briefly examine "The Lord's Prayer" that Jesus shared with His disciples. I've written a poem referring to "the Lord's Prayer" from a cowboy's perspective, which I identify with wholeheartedly. I urge you to focus on the majesty of our Father in heaven and be thankful for His unequaled grace and love in our lives.

THE COWBOY'S PRAYER

Dear Lord, God in heaven, from my bedroll on the
        ground—
I can't help but see Your majesty in the stars sparkling
        all around.
Your Good Book says You have a name for every star I
        see above;
I know You're looking at me too, for I can feel Your
        love.

Now some people dress in fancy clothes and call upon
        the Lord,

And some folks fill a pew up front, but sleep because
    they're bored.
I prefer to talk to You astride a sure-enough good, stout
    steed;
Ridin' across a prairie, Lord, Your company is all I need.

Lord, I thank You that You've put me here with a job I
    love to do;
Never was much on schoolin', thought I'd leave the
    thinking mostly up to You.
You've taught me right from wrong and how to work
    upon this land;
You've fed my family, warmed our home, and made our
    lives so grand.

Lord, let me work honest and strong for the wages I
    draw today;
There's so much more to life than what I bring home in
    my pay.
I know there will be food on our table, we've never
    gone hungry yet;
You've been the provider of all our needs from the very
    first day we met.

Forgive me, Lord, when I do the things I know I
    should not do,
And if I hurt a man with what I say, remind me those
    words were not from You.
Please search the thoughts I never speak and also search
    my heart;
Make me as clean as clean can be, just like I was at the
    very start.

Many a man has done me wrong, few times have I
    been treated fair;
I know You said forgive them all and, dear God, make
    this my prayer.
But Lord, it's so hard to forget every hurt that I've got
    stored up inside;
By Your power and love, I forgive them right now, and
    bury my own selfish pride.

Lord, keep me safe on this trail I ride, and if sometimes
    I drift from Your plan;
Guide me back gently to the land that I love, with the
    touch of Your awesome big hand.
The stars up above, I know You named every one, and I
    see my name written there;
One day I'll ride home, peace and joy for my own,
    with not one single worry or care.

While the American cowboy may not be the most educated and eloquent individual in our society, I hope you will appreciate some valuable insight on prayer from his point of view. Prayer has been, from the beginning of time, the principal means by which men and women, created in the image of God, have expressed their dependence on Him for everything. No one has ever understood this better than the American cowboy. Daniel Webster described prayer as "an approach to deity in word or thought, an earnest request, the act of praying to God." A cowboy, in his typically simplistic manner, would probably just say, "Prayer is talking and listening to God."

A Very Special Prayer

Our Father who is in heaven, hallowed be Your name
(Matthew 6:9).

Dear Lord, God in heaven, from my bedroll on the
ground—
I can't help but see Your majesty in the stars sparkling all
around.
Your Good Book says You have a name for every star I see
above;
I know You're looking at me too, for I can feel Your love.

Cowboys at the turn of the century had a very special feeling about God, and today's cowboys still do. They understand the vastness of nature, the elements they faced daily, and the importance of spending time alone in the presence of the Almighty. If it didn't rain, their livestock suffered. If it rained too much, it meant several days in a wet saddle trying to save their livelihood from perilous waters. As they climbed into their musty canvas bedrolls at night and gazed at millions of stars above, they had no problem realizing their smallness in the Lord's great creation and their total dependence upon His guiding hand.

The long and often dangerous cattle trails didn't leave a cowboy much time for being with his family, much less attending church. His bedroll was often the loneliest of places, filled with the knowledge of everything he left behind to pursue his dream of riding the open range and punching cattle. On many nights he gazed into the galaxy flat on his back. As he peered into infinity, he could almost smell his mother's hot apple pie and the scent of his dad's smokehouse. How he often longed to be home, enjoying a Sunday afternoon picnic under the big shade tree in their backyard.

My granddad shared many stories with me about his life as a cowboy. While everything within his being wanted to be a real-life, full-grown cowboy, he was only 17 when he left home, and he sure did miss his family. He said he could never forget his mama's tears as he rode away to join his first cattle drive. His daddy just turned his back and walked toward the barn like he had something really important to tend to while reaching up to rub something from his eyes.

Granddad thought of his family every night while he was on the trail. He wondered if his little sister was sitting by the upstairs window braiding her hair by the lantern light just like Mama had taught her. He was almost certain his little brother was listening as Grandpa Williams softly picked "Amazing Grace" on his guitar while sitting in his rocker on the front porch just before bedtime.

One night, just prior to dozing off to sleep, Granddad was startled from his dreams when a hawk screeched from the night sky above. His eyes were filled with a million blinking stars as the promise he made to his mother before he left home echoed in his mind: He would never let a night go by without saying his prayers, and this night would be no exception. He began to softly utter the prayer his mother had taught him as a boy: "Our Father who is in heaven" was all he managed to say. The young cowboy became overwhelmed by the magnitude of the universe spread out above him. As his eyes searched the sky from left to right as far as he could see, he wondered, "How big must God be to create all this?" While he lay there flat on his back he remembered a Bible story my great-grandmother had told him on a similar night a long, long time before. He thought it was from Isaiah, in the Old Testament, somewhere around chapter 40.

Lying there staring at the stars, curiosity finally got the best of him. As Cookie and the rest of the cowboys were snoring beneath their canvas bags, he borrowed a lantern from the chuck wagon, pulled a dry match from the chuck drawer, and soon had enough light to locate his grandpa's tattered old Bible in his saddle bags. Fumbling through the dog-eared, onionskin pages in the dim light, he finally found Isaiah. The story was coming back to him. He recalled how his grandmother always loved the little baby lambs that were born every spring on their ranch. But being a cowboy, Granddad preferred cows to sheep any day. Sheep cried too much and weren't very smart. He said they were so dumb they would follow each other right over the edge of a cliff until all were hopelessly lost.

Reading on, he realized that God tends His flock like a shepherd. He gathers the lambs in His arms and carries them close to His heart, gently leading those that have young. The same God that made all the stars in the sky loves even the smallest, dumbest, and smelliest of creatures.

He read Isaiah 40:12: "Who has measured the waters in the hollow of His hand," he suddenly realized that God is big—really big. God can hold all the waters on the earth in the hollow of His hand! What the prophet Isaiah and the cowboy didn't know then that we know now, is how much water there is on our planet.

Today there are five major oceans in our world. The Atlantic Ocean alone is said to measure approximately 33,420,000 square miles and hold 85 million cubic miles of water. A cubic mile measures one mile wide, by one mile deep, by one mile high, and equals more than one trillion gallons. The Pacific Ocean is comprised of some 141 million cubic miles of water. All the water on the earth measures some 326 million cubic miles of water, according to scientists.

> When I can't ride anymore, I shall still keep horses as long as I can hobble about with a bucket and a wheelbarrow. When I can't hobble, I shall roll my wheelchair out to the fence of the field where my horses graze, and watch them.
>
> MONICA DICKENS

The second half of Isaiah 40:12 reads, "…or with the breadth of his hands marked off the heavens" (NIV). As Granddad held his hand up toward the night sky, he was amazed by the immensity of the galaxy. He told me that as many nights as he'd spent outside, he'd never noticed how many stars there were in the sky.

Today's science tells us that our earth is some 25,000 miles in circumference and 8,000 miles in diameter. However, earth is only a part of the small galaxy we know as the Milky Way containing billions of stars. If we were to travel from one side of the Milky Way to the other at the speed of light (186,000 miles per second), it would take 100,000 years. There are 20 galaxies in our corner of the universe. It would take 2.5 million years to travel through those galaxies at the speed of light. Many scientists believe there are more than a billion galaxies, each with 100 billion stars. Psalm 147:4-5 reads, "[The LORD] counts the number of the stars; He gives names to all of them. Great is our Lord and abundant in strength; His understanding is infinite." Just as sure as it was difficult for my granddad to understand the magnitude of God, we too should stand in awe of God's limitless wisdom and power.

While we may not be able to totally grasp the complexity of God, we can identify with the reality of His love. The God who chose to create everything and name every star in the universe did so simply because He is love. Every person was created in the image of God and has the ability to reflect His character. Jesus said we should address God as "Our Father in heaven." Mere words can't express what a privilege it is to be part of the family of God and to talk personally with the Creator of the universe as one of His beloved children.

While God is both holy and majestic, He is also loving and personally interested in His family. The apostle Paul describes God: "The God who made the world and everything in it is the Lord of heaven and earth…From one man he made all the nations, that they should inhabit the whole earth; and he marked out their appointed times in history and the boundaries of their lands. God did this so that they would seek him and perhaps reach out for him and find him" (Acts 17:24,26-28 NIV).

If my granddad were here today, he would tell you from experience that the God who created all things—every single star in the sky, every drop of water in every ocean, every cute little lamb, and every cowboy who ever saddled a horse—desires that no person should perish, that all would come to know Him as their "Father who is in heaven."

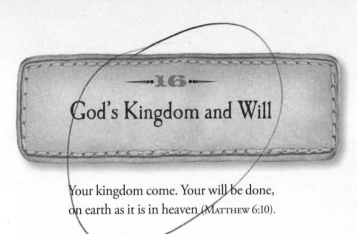

God's Kingdom and Will

Your kingdom come. Your will be done,
on earth as it is in heaven (Matthew 6:10).

Lord, I thank You that You've put me here with a job I
    love to do;
Never was much on schoolin', thought I'd leave the
    thinking mostly up to You.
You've taught me right from wrong and how to work
    upon this land;
You've fed my family, warmed our home, and made our
    lives so grand.

God, through the Holy Spirit, is present in the hearts of everyone whom He calls His children. When we pray that God's will be done, we pray that His perfect purpose will be accomplished in this world and throughout eternity. As children of God, we know that He loves and cares for us personally. He wants us to see His will fulfilled in our lives.

I like what John Wayne once said: "There's right and there's wrong. You get to do one or the other. You do one and you're living. You do the other, and you may be walking around but you're as dead as a beaver hat." Now that's a little cowboy logic that's easy to understand. When we choose to walk outside the boundaries God has ordained in our lives, we usually suffer disappointment. When we are not in His perfect will, we are not able to successfully contribute to His kingdom.

About 25 years ago, I had an opportunity to do something right, as John Wayne put it, and in doing so, I was incredibly blessed. I was a young, aspiring western artist making a living as a part-time cowboy, raising a couple of horses and a few cows, and day-working whenever I could for a few extra bucks to buy art supplies. It was Christmas Eve, and my family and I were going through some rather difficult financial times. The afternoon mail brought me a Christmas card from my parents with a crisp $100 bill neatly tucked inside. What marvelous timing since I didn't have enough money to buy many presents for our family. It was getting late and the stores would be closing early, so I quickly headed my pickup toward town.

It was very cold that December afternoon, and the wind was blowing hard out of the north. A light dusting of snow still covered the ground from the night before. Just before I made the turn off our road toward town, I passed the small, wood-frame ranch house that was surrounded by brush and scrubby trees. It sat back off the farm-to-market road about 100 yards and was hard to see unless you were really looking for it. I had briefly met the cowhand and his family who lived there several months back, and I often waved at the children playing outside in the yard when I drove by.

As I sped past the house, I saw two little girls and a boy playing in the front yard. At that moment, I felt an overwhelming sense that God wanted me to stop. I didn't want to because I had important Christmas shopping to do, so I kept driving. But about a mile down the road the feeling intensified, so I turned around and went back to the house. I sensed that God had something more important to accomplish.

When I got out of the car, the entire family came over to greet me. One little girl asked me if I wanted to see their Christmas decorations. I said yes, and she took me by the hand. We all went inside the dilapidated old farmhouse. It was adorned for the season in an array of construction paper decorations and strings of popcorn hung from the cedar tree they'd cut from their pasture. While it was a very heartwarming experience, I couldn't help but notice it was freezing cold in the house. They had no fireplace, and they admitted they didn't have enough money to replace the old woodstove that had rusted out the year before. All the water in the house was frozen, and everyone kept bundled in coats and blankets day and night to stay warm. The five children ranged in age from two years to seven, and I was concerned for their safety.

As I drove away, the family stood on the front porch and waved. I knew I had heard from God. I thought if I hurried, I might find them a little electric heater that would give them enough heat for the night, and I would still have enough time and money left to do some Christmas shopping for my family. It was now almost four o'clock, and most of the stores in our little town would be closed because it was Christmas

> Good judgment comes from experience, and a lot of that comes from bad judgment.
>
> COWBOY WISDOM

Eve. As I was heading to the mall, I passed a flea market. Standing in the middle of the parking lot in front of the store was a big, black wood-stove with a sign on it that read $100. The writing was on the wall. You can probably surmise what happened next.

The children's father and I had the new stove installed just before dark and enough wood from our house stacked by theirs to last through the holidays. They were so thankful for a warm Christmas. One of the young girls told me later it was the best Christmas they'd ever had. It was certainly one of the best for me.

The very next morning around eight, we heard a knock at our front door. I gazed out the window and was surprised to see my Sunday school teacher, Ray Lewis, standing on the porch. As I opened the door, he said, "Merry Christmas!" and handed me an envelope. Inside was a check for almost $150. He said our class had taken up a collection and wanted us to have it. I learned that day how God's kingdom is alive in the hearts of His people and how God uses people just like you and me to carry out His perfect will.

Like John Wayne said, it is good to do the right thing!

17

Daily Bread

Give us this day our daily bread
(MATTHEW 6:11).

Lord, let me work honest and strong for the wages I
    draw today;
There's so much more to life than what I bring home in
    my pay.
I know there will be food on our table, we've never
    gone hungry yet;
You've been the provider of all our needs from the very
    first day we met.

God is the provider of everything we need. It is through His great love for us that He sustains us daily. "Our daily bread" refers to everything necessary to sustain our lives. I believe it not only applies to our physical lives, but to our spiritual lives as well. Jesus refers to Himself as "the bread of life" (John 6:35). And it is through our sacramental communion with the bread that we are reminded of His great sacrifice on the cross at Calvary. I'm not proud to admit that there have been times in my life when I've taken pride in the fact that I was "self-made, strong, and independent," so I believed I didn't need any help from anyone. Because I was focused on me and not on the holiness and majesty of God, I failed to realize that everything I have and all that I am is a result of God's perfect provision.

There have been so many times in my life where I can look back and see how God provided exactly what I needed, when I needed it. Sometimes God even gave me far more than what I needed. One such time was during the energy crisis in the 1980s, and very few people were buying western art. I really needed some customers since most of the oil money in Texas had dried up. I had to sell some art quick or get a "real" job. My wife decided I should think about going back to work on a ranch since I loved the life of a cowboy so much. The money wasn't that great, but at least the work would be steady.

It was a big weekend in town because the Texas State Arts & Crafts Fair was going on. Thousands of tourists came from all over Texas and neighboring states to visit the three-day event. A local gallery owner rented a big, red-and-white tent, tied balloons and banners all over it, spread hay bales throughout, and hung 29 of my paintings. We were set up on the busiest street corner in town. Believe me, everybody saw us. I must admit I felt more like a circus clown than a cowboy artist, but I was desperate.

Friday night came, and we had a lot of lookers but no one bought anything. Most everyone who came were locals who made circus jokes at our expense. We showed up bright and early Saturday morning, confidently dressed in our finest western apparel, ready to put a painting in the trunk of the first 29 cars that showed up. You see, a truly seasoned artist must be an eternal optimist. Once again, we had a lot of lookers but no takers. Not even one measly offer. By mid-afternoon Saturday, my confidence was waning. Some friends from church stopped by to lend moral support. They'd been praying for months for our business to improve, and on this day they prayed for new customers to come to the show and buy every single painting we had. My faith was weak. I thought as they prayed how happy I would be to just sell one.

Right before we were ready to load up late that afternoon, with not one sale for the entire weekend, a man and his wife strolled into the tent. They were in town from Iowa and said they wanted to buy some authentic western art. After about a half hour of looking at and discussing my paintings, the man said, "If I buy them all, will you deliver them to Des Moines?" I'm sure you can guess my answer! Despite my lack of faith that afternoon, God provided so much more than my daily bread. What had begun as an embarrassment for a young artist in need of encouragement, ended up a blessing and a significant turning point in my career.

"Our daily bread" is the very sustenance we need to fulfill God's will for our lives here on earth. All we have to do is put our faith in Him, and He will provide. He always has and He always will.

18

Forgive Us as We Forgive

Forgive us our debts, as we also have
forgiven our debtors (Matthew 6:12).

Forgive me, Lord, when I do the things I know I
   should not do;
And if I hurt a man with what I say, remind me those
   words were not from You.
Please search the thoughts I never speak and also search
   my heart;
Make me as clean as clean can be, just like I was at the
   very start.

Many a man has done me wrong, few times have I
   been treated fair;
I know You said forgive them all and, dear God, make
   this my prayer.
But Lord, it's so hard to forget every hurt that I've got
   stored up inside;
By Your power and love, I forgive them right now, and
   bury my own selfish pride.

Forgiveness is a top priority with God. Jesus mentions the importance of forgiveness in His model prayer, and emphasizes the necessity of *total* forgiveness: "If you forgive others for their transgressions, your heavenly Father will also forgive you. But if you do not forgive others, then your Father will not forgive your transgressions" (Matthew 6:14-15).

Can you imagine the God who named every star and holds all the water on our planet in the cup of His hands not forgiving you? When we do not forgive others as God has forgiven us, we deny that we are sinners in need of His forgiveness. But in God's eyes, we are all alike. He created each individual in His image that we might be reflections of His glory. He loves every single being and item He created, and "the Lord is not slow in keeping his promise, as some understand slowness. Instead he is patient with you, not wanting anyone to perish, but everyone to come to repentance" (2 Peter 3:9 NIV).

For most of us, it is easy to ask God for forgiveness but it's hard to forgive others. Peter had asked Jesus, "Lord, how often shall my brother sin against me and I forgive him? Up to seven times?" When Peter asked this, he knew the Jewish rabbis taught it was necessary to forgive people three times if they offend you. In his attempt to be generous, Peter had changed this to seven times. Jesus replied that we should forgive people who truly repent every time they ask—the very same way God forgives us. If we choose not to forgive, we separate ourselves from the fellowship of God's love (see the parable of the unforgiving debtor in Matthew 18:21-35). The choice is ours to make.

An old-time cowboy in West Texas told me a story of a cattle drive he rode on when he was a young man. Bill had worked for several years alongside six other cowboys for Buddy Johnson on a large ranch known as the Bar 7. Even though Bill was very young, Mr. Johnson chose him to be the trail boss on the cattle drive from Texas to Kansas. This caused some jealousy among the other cowboys. Bill had proven himself to be a good, dependable cowboy, and he was as honest as they came. Mr. Johnson had quite a reputation as a good judge of character from his service in the Civil War, and he knew Bill was the best man for the job.

Mr. Johnson ran about 700 head on the Bar 7, and he wanted to get them to market before winter set in up north. He rode with the cowboys every mile of the way to keep an eye on his sizeable investment. He dispatched Bill out ahead of the herd to scout good places to make camp near water and to be on the guard for rustlers or unfriendly Indians. Bill often had to ride two or more days out and then back again to find suitable spots to rest the cows.

It was necessary not to move the herd too fast in the heat because they would lose too much weight. The stockyards paid for beef by the pound, so great care was taken not to push them too fast and to make sure they had plenty to eat and drink. Bill performed his duties flawlessly and with great pride. The cattle were moved an average of ten miles a day, and almost every night they camped by water. The cows always seemed to be calmer near the water and rested better through the night.

While the cows were moving calmly along and the weather was being cooperative, some of the other cowboys were becoming increasingly jealous of Bill. Mr. Johnson paid them little attention, and they felt like they were doing all the work while Bill rode out leisurely in search of new campsites. While they were ridin' drag and eatin' dust during the day and supping on beans at night, they wrongly speculated that Bill was living it up in town somewhere. They spent their evenings scheming up ways to get rid of Bill. If they could cut Bill out of his share, it meant more money for all of them come payday.

Bill had set up camp that night along the banks of a river. The chuck wagon fire was growing dim and all but the night-herding cowboys were in their bedrolls. Suddenly a loud crash of lightning dropped from the northern sky above. It was the first cold front of the year, and it was going to be a big one. Thunder and lightning crashed all around. Every cowboy jumped from his bedroll and headed for his horse. This was stampede weather.

The cattle, aroused from their sleep, were up on their feet, nervously moving about. Bill was the first cowboy to be horseback and worked to make his way to the cattle closest to the river. He knew if there was a stampede, he had to turn them away from the water or many would drown in the mash of bodies. But before he could reach the lead steer, another bolt of lightning crashed to the ground. The cattle bolted! Bill rode headlong into the river. He thought if he crossed before the cattle, he could turn the leader back, leaving the other cowboys in position to head them off and eventually calm them down. Bill's horse was a good swimmer, and he was sure he could beat the cows to the other side. By that time, most of the cowboys were horseback, but they could do nothing to stop the herd. They were too late, and Mr. Johnson yelled for them to stay away from the water and the thundering body of animals.

Suddenly Bill's horse dropped about a foot and couldn't keep his head above water. It was quicksand, and there was nothing Bill

could do in the fast current unless someone threw him a rope. Frantically looking over his shoulder toward camp, he could see three cowboys watching him. He yelled for a rope, but no one reached for his lariat. *Maybe they can't hear me,* he thought. But then from behind the cowboys rode Mr. Johnson, swinging his rope above the heads of the stampeding cattle and out toward Bill. Bill managed to catch it and dallied it around the saddle horn. With his horse fighting to get out of the sand and struggling desperately to breathe, Bill signaled his boss and yelled, "Pull!"

With his horse too tired to fight, Bill had to make a decision. He could tie the rope around himself and be pulled to safety or jump off and hopefully reduce the burden enough so his horse could break free and be pulled ashore. By this time, all the cowboys were watching. Bill leaped from his saddle into the raging river and disappeared into the darkness. Mr. Johnson's horse managed to pull the other horse free, and soon everyone was searching for Bill.

Most of the storm front had blown through and the lightning had subsided when one of the cowboys found Bill several hundred yards down river, where he'd finally managed to swim to the bank. He was exhausted, but his first question was about his horse. "Did you save him?" The cowboy nodded and helped Bill back to camp.

Cookie had the fire started by the time they returned, and everyone gathered 'round. The cattle had disappeared into the night and would have to be rounded up. But now was not the time. Mr. Johnson sternly asked the cowboys why they hadn't helped Bill. Every wet Stetson pointed toward the ground, and no one uttered a word. Just then a tired, wet, skinny young cowboy stood up and said, "Don't worry, fellers. I probably would have done the same thing if I were in your boots. How about we saddle up and go get them cows?"

It took a lot of courage for Bill to say that. Looking beyond the young cowboy's simple words, what was he really saying? "I forgive each one of you cowboys. I know you did me wrong, but I probably would've done the same thing if I were in your boots. Now we have a job to do, and it takes every single one of us to do it. So saddle up and let's ride." Bill knew unless he completely forgave them, they would never be able to work together to get the cattle to market on time. He also understood the jealousy the other cowboys had for him. He'd felt the same way just a few short years ago. Youthful ambition sometimes blinds people's vision from the truth.

And, friends, we have a choice just like Bill did. Do we sink or swim? We can choose to forgive and be forgiven or we can choose not to forgive and be separated from the fellowship of God.

19

Protect Us from Evil

Do not lead us into temptation, but
deliver us from evil (Matthew 6:13).

Lord, keep me safe on this trail I ride, and if sometimes
    I drift from Your plan;
Guide me back gently to the land that I love, with the
    touch of Your awesome big hand.
The stars up above, I know You named every one, and I
    see my name written there;
One day I'll ride home, peace and joy for my own,
    with not one single worry or care.

While God does not lead us into temptation, He some times allows those whom He loves to be tested. My dad always says it builds character. Even Jesus was tempted by Satan, just as we are today. All of us struggle with temptations of one sort or another, but God assures us, "No temptation has overtaken you except what is common to mankind. And God is faithful; he will not let you be tempted beyond what you can bear. But when you are tempted, he will also provide a way out so that you can endure it" (1 Corinthians 10:13 NIV).

This brings to mind a fine old cowboy from New Mexico. He wrangled on some of the best ranches in New Mexico and Arizona all of his life. Jim Wescott was forced to hang up his spurs a few years ago because the strenuous life as a working cowboy had finally taken its toll. After many broken bones, bruises, and near-death experiences, he now sits and reminisces of days gone by.

Jim often shares how jobs were scarce for cowboys because ranch owners had a very difficult time making ends meet through the droughts, economic depressions, and diseases. A young cowboy who had not yet gained a reputation in the saddle often had to prove himself before he was signed on permanently. Money was too hard to come by to waste on a man who wasn't worth his salt. If he was lucky enough to be hired, 1946 wages were $90 a month, plus a cot in the bunkhouse and three meals a day. Jim recalls how he was put to the test on his first job on the Panama Ranch in the Guadalupe Mountains of New Mexico.

Ranch owners and foremen were not always sure of new cowboys. They wanted to test their abilities with a rope and in the saddle. Oftentimes they paired the new cowboy with the rankest horse in the outfit—the one nobody wanted to ride. Jim recalls how the owner told him, "If you can ride the night horse in the morning, you can work for the Panama." Jim could hardly wait until morning. This young cowboy was sure there had never been a horse he couldn't ride. *Getting this job will be a cinch,* he thought.

The night horse was the animal kept in the corral to use to wrangle the other horses from the pasture before work began in the morning. The wrangler's job was to rise from his bunk long before daylight, saddle the night horse, and gather the rest of the remuda before breakfast. The horses were penned just before sunup in the corral, so they'd be ready to be saddled for the day's work.

The Panama had a dozen or so horses that hadn't been saddle broke. The boss had fired the last wrangler, and none of the other cowboys in the outfit had the ability or inclination to tame the horses and teach them to accept a saddle and direction from a rider. There was one horse in the bunch that was particularly mean-spirited. No one had been able to ride him. The owner had named him Satan.

The Panama's owner decided it would be interesting to switch the night horse with Satan to see how young Jim would handle him in the morning. He would put the young cowboy to the test to find out if he had the makings of a wrangler.

Jim turned in right after supper so he'd be ready for his big opportunity. Most of the other cowboys didn't have much to say to him anyway since he was new. They seldom welcomed a stranger until he'd proven himself to be a good hand. Jim crawled out of his bedroll long before daylight. He threw his saddle over one shoulder and carried the saddle blanket and bridle in the other hand. His spurs jingled through the darkness as he walked toward the corral where the night horse waited.

By the time he'd walked the 50-some yards to the corral, he noticed a light on in the main ranch house. He could see the owner silhouetted in front of the window on the veranda and several cowboys standing nearby. *This is unusual,* he thought. Most of them would normally sleep for another 30 minutes or more. Nevertheless, he had a job to do. Jim opened the corral gate and went about his business.

He had no sooner latched the gate behind him before the big brown horse in the corral reared up and pawed the air with his front legs. Landing on all fours, the cayuse headed toward Jim. At that moment the cowboy figured he'd been set up. In a split second he realized he had two choices. He could either quit and move on to another ranch or fight for the job he wanted and prove himself. He heard the cowboys chuckling from the veranda. He was tempted to gather his things and ride off, but he grabbed his lariat and caught Satan around the neck. After a dust-filled fight around the corral, he choked him down and slipped the bridle over his head.

> No hour of life is wasted that is spent in the saddle.
>
> WINSTON CHURCHILL

Jim threw the blanket and then the saddle on the horse's back with one hand. He cinched it down, keeping a tight hold on the reins with his other hand. Putting one foot in the stirrup, he flung himself up on Satan's back and the rodeo began. "After 10 or 12 seconds of bucking, jumping, twisting, and snorting, Satan throwed me higher than the saddle-house roof," Jim said. But that ride was longer than anyone else had ever stayed on the bronc's back. The cowboys cheered as Jim scraped himself off the corral floor and gathered his tack.

The boss came over to the corral and offered Jim his hand. "Son, my wife's fixin' steak, gravy, and biscuits with syrup. Come on over to

the house, and let's have some breakfast. The horses won't mind waiting a while."

Jim made quite an impression on the boss and the other cowboys.
And he got his first paying job as a cowboy. He soon received an additional $25 a month for breaking horses. He not only passed the test,
but his attitude became an example to the other cowboys on the ranch.

Many times in life we're faced with trials and temptations just like
Jim was. Sometimes we are deceived; sometimes we are simply weak.
We're all human, and we all make mistakes. Thankfully, our Father in
heaven has lovingly provided a way out for us. As we pray for God to
deliver us from evil, it is essential to remember the provisions He has
already made on our behalf to ensure our victory! All we have to do
is appropriate them. It is our responsibility to pray, to resist temptation, and, finally to fight the spiritual forces that seek to destroy us by
calling on Jesus. Just as young Jim had his chaps, boots, bridle, saddle, and lariat to deal with Satan, we too are promised in the Bible that
God will provide protective armor for us to use to safely do battle (see
Ephesians 6).

Timothy tells us to flee from youthful lusts and unrighteousness.
But sometimes we must stand up and fight for what is right. As we
pursue and model the qualities of holiness that God reserved for His
children, God may bless us by giving us the responsibility to help others
find salvation through His Son, Jesus Christ. Yes, we can learn a lot
from the life of cowboy Jim Wescott. He was tempted to quit, but
he resisted and fought back with all his skill and might. And he was
rewarded for his actions.

Part 3

WIDE OPEN SPACES

Growing Up in the Great Outdoors

Most folks find nature and the great outdoors fascinating. My fascination with them began in early childhood. The simplicity of whiling away the time skipping rocks across a shallow pond with some pals or climbing trees and playing king of the jungle brought so much pleasure. Some of my fondest memories are of driving close to a fishing spot, and then spending the hot summer days trampling over dusty, crimson rocks and sand, dodging thorny mesquite limbs, and keeping one step behind my grandmother on the way to one of her "sure enough" good catfish holes.

My uncle Billy Bob always tagged along, toting our poles and certain to get some fishing line tangled into a web of unusable proportions while muttering muffled frustrations under his breath. He often tripped over the dangling mess he'd created and would find himself entangled in a dusty pile of debris among the rocks and cactus. Oh, the joys of fishing! What a time the three of us had together!

When we finally arrived at the fishing hole and got our bait into the water, we would sit back on the bank and enjoy the day. Red-tailed hawks and buzzards circled in the sky above us, while jackrabbits with long, erect ears stood like statues in the shade of prickly pear cacti. The now-almost-extinct horned toads, looking like miniature dinosaurs, crawled tirelessly across the cracked, red ground in search of ants and other insects to devour. Grandmother reminisced about the old times, and just when I was completely enthralled in one of her stories, a bobber would sink! The water would splash as we caught up a pole, set the hook, and fought with the big one on the line. By the end of the day, we'd have a stringer full of catfish almost as big as the smile on my face.

After fishing, Grandmother always let me drive her Buick sedan down the rural dirt roads until we reached the blacktop leading to her house. Once home, we enjoyed fried catfish as the sweet reward for a good day's work. When the stars began to sparkle, it was off for a bath and just one more story before our perfect day came to a close. My fond dreams of the big one that didn't get away were interrupted by the sunlight of a new day filled with even greater expectations.

My grandmother loved to go fishing because she understood life's simple pleasures. She saw the beauty of the great outdoors as a gift from God to be enjoyed and shared. She savored every moment. I'm very thankful she passed that great heritage down to me.

> If we truly love people, we will desire for them far more than it is within our power to give them, and this will lead us to prayer. Intercession is a way of loving others.
>
> RICHARD FOSTER

Through the years, I've been privileged to hunt elk in the wilderness of the Rocky Mountains, ducks in the swamps of East Texas, and trophy deer in the thick brush of South Texas. I've fished for bull reds in the Gulf of Mexico and northern pike in the frigid waters of Canada. I've hiked to the tops of majestic waterfalls in Yosemite National Park and flown between the towering rock walls of the Grand Canyon. I've watched the leaves change colors right before my eyes in the rolling hills of Maine.

A trip to New England encouraged me to ponder some aspects about the great outdoors from a different perspective. I discovered I'd been taking the freedom of nature for granted. While I've immensely enjoyed my many adventures, I'd lost sight of what a privilege having the opportunities to truly enjoy such things was. On this particular trip, I was reminded of the history of our great nation and the sacrifice the early settlers made so we might enjoy our freedoms. For several evenings, I sat watching the sunset on the harbor of the quaint fishing village of Camden, Maine. I thought about the schooners with their masts docked below, and how the early pilgrims spent many perilous months at sea as they pursued American soil. The freedom we have today to experience this wonderful country came at a high cost. We are indeed blessed!

With much gratitude to God, America's founding fathers, my family, and my teachers, I'm excited to share with you some of my observations and experiences in the great Alaskan wilderness. For six amazing days I was totally overwhelmed by the handiwork of God. Because mere words can't accurately express my feelings and what I discovered, I urge you to draw from your own personal experiences as you read. Bask for a few moments in the wonderful world of the great outdoors. It is a very special gift from God to be shared and enjoyed by each of us…and the generations to come.

In the Beginning

How often we take the world around us for granted. As the pressures and deadlines of society continually pull us in all directions, it can be difficult to enjoy life's beautiful surroundings. If we only slow down and open our eyes, we will find a glorious world has been created for us to enjoy.

God created the magnificent planet Earth, where we are blessed to live. This orb supplies all our physical needs plus great beauty and pleasure. When we stand in awe of snow-covered peaks, roaring waterfalls, crystal-clear streams, turquoise-blue oceans, and satellite images of our universe, we are merely observing a portion of the beauty and holiness of God Himself.

David wrote these beautiful words:

> LORD, our Lord, how majestic is your name in all the earth! You have set your glory in the heavens…When I consider your heavens, the work of your fingers, the moon and the stars, which you have set in place, what is mankind that you are mindful of them, human beings that you care for them? You have made them a little lower than the angels and crowned them with glory and honor. You made them rulers over the works of your hands; you put everything under their feet: all flocks and herds, and the animals of the wild, the birds in the sky, and the fish in the sea, all that swim the paths of the seas. LORD, our Lord, how majestic is your name in all the earth! (Psalm 8:1,3-9).

Perhaps that is the reason mankind has from the beginning of time dared to climb the highest mountains, explore outer space, and venture to the bottom of the world's oceans. Whether you enjoy rock climbing, scuba diving, hunting, fishing, horseback riding, cycling, bird-watching, golf, or just an afternoon picnic in a field clothed in wild flowers, the glory of God is all around.

Genesis 1:1 says, "In the beginning God created the heavens and the earth." Contained in this simple verse are more facts than my limited mind can comprehend. Science can tell us many things about our

universe that causes me to simply stand in overwhelming awe at God's power and creativity. The galaxy we live in is spinning at the speed of 490,000 miles per hour, but it still needs 200 million years to complete one rotation. Astronomers estimate our galaxy contains more than 30 billion suns, many of which are larger than our own, which is more than 1.5 million times larger than earth. Our galaxy, the Milky Way, is thought to be 200,000 light-years in diameter. Light travels at 186,000 miles per second. Scientists believe there is considerably more beyond it.

How truly incredible God is! How infinitely beautiful is our universe! It's hard for me to comprehend that some people believe our world and all its life came into existence almost accidentally. A glorious palette filled with infinite colors paints our earthly home and the heavens above in this masterpiece from God's brush. The apostle Paul wrote, "Since the creation of the world God's invisible qualities—his eternal power and divine nature—have been clearly seen, being understood from what has been made, so that people are without excuse" (Romans 1:20). If we can't see God's power and understand His nature through all He has created, perhaps it is time to put our busy schedules aside and spend a few days in the great outdoors.

Jesus enjoyed the great outdoors during His years on earth. He spent time alone in the desert, on mountains, and in gardens. He had a particular fondness for the sea. He prayed on the sea, walked on seawater, preached from the sea, and fed multitudes using the sea's bounty. He also had a heart for fishermen. One day while walking by the Sea of Galilee, He chose a group of fishermen to be among His disciples. These outdoorsmen understood the concept of casting nets. Jesus said to them, "Come, follow me...and I will send you out to fish for people" (Matthew 4:19).

Jesus understood the concept of fishing and knew enjoying good company, beautiful surroundings, and good food here on earth was a reflection of the larger spiritual event to come. As He fellowshipped with His friends in the great outdoors, He invited all of humankind to fellowship with Him in the glorious surroundings of His heavenly home and to eat food from His heavenly table. His invitation still stands today!

> Praise the LORD, my soul.
> LORD my God, you are very great;
>   you are clothed with splendor and majesty.
> The LORD wraps himself in light as with a garment;
>   he stretches out the heavens like a tent
>   and lays the beams of his upper chambers on their
>   waters.
> He makes the clouds his chariot
>   and rides on the wings of the wind.
> He set the earth on its foundations;
>   it can never be moved.
> You covered it with the watery depths as with a garment;
>   the waters stood above the mountains.
> But at your rebuke the waters fled,
>   at the sound of your thunder they took to flight;
>   they flowed over the mountains,

they went down into the valleys,
    to the place you assigned for them.
You set a boundary they cannot cross;
    never again will they cover the earth.
He makes springs pour water into the ravines;
    it flows between the mountains.
They give water to all the beasts of the field;
    the wild donkeys quench their thirst.
The birds of the sky nest by the waters;
    they sing among the branches.
He waters the mountains from his upper chambers;
    the land is satisfied by the fruit of his work.
He makes grass grow for the cattle,
    and plants for people to cultivate—
    bringing forth food from the earth:
    wine that gladdens human hearts,
    oil to make their faces shine,
    and bread that sustains their hearts.
The trees of the LORD are well watered,
    the cedars of Lebanon that he planted.
There the birds make their nests;
    the stork has its home in the junipers.
The high mountains belong to the wild goats;
    the crags are a refuge for the hyrax.
He made the moon to mark the seasons,
    and the sun knows when to go down.
You bring darkness, it becomes night,
    and all the beasts of the forest prowl.
The lions roar for their prey
    and seek their food from God.
The sun rises, and they steal away;
    they return and lie down in their dens.
Then people go out to their work,
    to their labor until evening.

How many are your works, Lord!
In wisdom you made them all;
    the earth is full of your creatures.
There is the sea, vast and spacious,
    teeming with creatures beyond number—
    living things both large and small.
There the ships go to and fro,
    and Leviathan, which you formed to frolic there.
All creatures look to you
    to give them their food at the proper time.
When you give it to them,
    they gather it up;
    when you open your hand,
    they are satisfied with good things.
When you hide your face,
    they are terrified;
    when you take away their breath,
    they die and return to the dust.
When you send your Spirit,
    they are created,
    and you renew the face of the ground.
May the glory of the Lord endure forever;
    may the Lord rejoice in his works—
    he who looks at the earth, and it trembles,
    who touches the mountains, and they smoke.
I will sing to the Lord all my life;
    I will sing praise to my God as long as I live.
May my meditation be pleasing to him,
    as I rejoice in the Lord.
But may sinners vanish from the earth
    and the wicked be no more.
Praise the Lord, my soul.
Praise the Lord (Psalm 104).

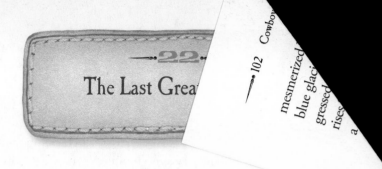

22. The Last Grea[t]

mesmerized
blue glaci
gressed
rises
a

though I have spent a great deal of time outdoors and visited many secluded places, I've never experienced the magnitude and glory of creation as in the Alaskan wilderness. Being from Texas, I understand the term "big," but Alaska is truly a territory like no other. It is a beautiful, rugged, and wild land of incredible towering mountains, slow-moving glaciers, active volcanoes, broad valleys, pristine lakes and rivers, hot springs and icy streams, rocky coastlines, waterfalls, dense coniferous forests, and an abundance of fish, birds, and other wildlife.

In the summer of my fiftieth year, I was invited to spend a week fly-fishing for migrating salmon with my lifelong friend and outdoorsman Rusty Pool in the wilderness on the Alaskan Peninsula. I knew very little about Alaska outside of Eskimos, igloos, and oil wells, so I jumped at the opportunity to see an area so few people have set foot on.

The word "Alaska" is derived from an Aleut word meaning "great land." The state is known as "the Last Frontier" because of its many opportunities and sparse population. The 2010 population census was around 710,000 for the entire state that has a total land area of 586,000 square miles. Alaska has more total area of lakes and rivers than any other state, equaling more than the entire land area of Massachusetts and Vermont combined. There are more than 100,000 glaciers in Alaska, some larger than the state of Rhode Island.

My first glimpse of the magnitude of the forty-ninth state was from a small airplane window some 30,000 feet above the grand landscape. All I could see for hours en route to King Salmon were the snow-covered mountains of the Alaska and Brooks Ranges. They seemed to travel endlessly in both directions as far as the eye could see. I was

by the expanse of the mountains and the size of the crystal-
ers frigidly nestled between the icy slopes. As the flight pro-
, I could see Mt. McKinley on the horizon far to the north. It
20,320 feet above sea level, almost four miles high, and towers like
giant over the surrounding mountains. Seventeen of the 20 largest
mountains in the United States are in Alaska. My excitement was build-
ing with the passing of each mile. I was beginning to grasp the enormity
of the wilderness below.

Much of Alaska is inaccessible by road due to the arduous landscape,
so the next phase of our journey would be a two-and-a-half-hour flight
from King Salmon to our camp on the Alaska Peninsula in a tiny four-passenger plane. At the helm of our rather ragged blue and rusty Cessna was a former military pilot who, like many others, had chosen to make a life for himself by flying people into the bush where few dared to venture.

The Alaska Peninsula is a rugged land filled with impressive beauty. It includes nearly 16 million acres, which is relatively small in comparison to the mainland. The mountains of the Aleutian Range comprise its backbone. The peninsula is composed of towering mountains, broad valleys, foggy fjords, and often steep and rocky coastlines. Glacial lakes, rich tundra, and 14 major volcanoes, including 9 that are still active, are scattered throughout the region. It is a habitat for 222 species of resident and migratory wildlife. The rangers at Becharof National Wildlife Refuge have calculated there are 30 species of terrestrial mammals, 11 species of marine mammals, 146 bird species, and 35 species of fish. Sea lions, otters, seals, seabirds, and waterfowl inhabit the coastal areas. Bald eagles, hawks, falcons, and

> Climb the mountains and get their good tidings.
> Nature's peace will flow into you as sunshine flows into trees
> The winds will blow their own freshness into you, and the storms their energy,
> While cares will drop off like autumn leaves.
>
> JOHN MUIR

owls nest on the rock pinnacles and spires along the coast. The tundra lowlands are host to caribou, moose, brown bear, wolves, swans, and other waterfowl. What an amazing place!

Brown or "grizzly" bears make use of all the land from the mountaintops to the coastline. They roam the tundra in search of roots, berries, ground squirrels, and other small burrowing animals when their preferred diet of salmon is unavailable.

Thousands of caribou migrate along the peninsula each year, just as their ancestors have for centuries. Unlike most species of deer, these animals spend their entire lives on the move.

To observe the Alaska Peninsula is like stepping back in time hundreds, even thousands, of years and viewing the earth as it was originally created—unspoiled by the hands of mankind, still raw and natural just as God designed it.

⟶ 23 ⟵

Our Home for the Week

Our flight into camp was a magnificent sight. We soared over hundreds of miles of winding rivers, lush green valleys, herds of caribou, dozens of large grizzly bears, bald eagles, and even the mouth of a steaming volcano.

As we began our descent on the south side of the volcano, I got my first glimpse of the Pacific Ocean on the southern horizon and knew we were approaching our final destination. Nakalilok Bay occupied the inlet between the ocean and the volcano and was surrounded by a horseshoe of lush green mountains and rolling hills. They were covered with tall, pink flowers known as fireweed and rather short, dense alder trees creating a heavy cover of brush—perfect habitat for bears. Rivers and streams crookedly flowed into the bay from the snowcapped peaks. I saw the tents of our camp perched on a steep hill along the shoreline overlooking the bay. As I peered down below us into the water, it suddenly occurred to me there was no place to land the plane. The hills were too steep and the narrow shoreline was covered with rocks and outcroppings.

Upon my rather loud inquisition, the seasoned pilot said, "Not to worry. I'll put her down right there." He pointed out the tiny window to a narrow stretch of beach along the base of a hill just north of camp and adjacent to the bay. I later found out that a plane is only able to land there when the tidewaters are out and in the absence of thick fog that frequently seeps into the bay from the Pacific Ocean. The tides seem to be rather unpredictable on the peninsula, and no one is able to accurately pinpoint their exact schedule. In the wilderness, there are no weather or radio stations, so much depends on the instincts and expertise of the pilot. Our landing went smoothly, and our guides for the weeklong adventure were there to greet us.

As we stepped off the plane, we immediately saw bear tracks in the wet sand. Upon a closer look, they were everywhere—and they were big. Leaving their imprints in long winding paths from the beach, the bears disappeared into the grassy hills beyond or around the craggy coastline. At that moment, I knew my dream of a true wilderness adventure had begun.

I couldn't believe the amount of cargo we unloaded from that small plane. It would have been a tight fit to cram it all into a Greyhound bus. The fact we even got off the ground was a miracle, I decided. After several trips up the steep, hand-hewn trail to camp with our gear and rations, we were ready to catch our breath and take in the sights around us.

The sky was baby-blue with a few white, billowy clouds. The air was so fresh I was certain no man or beast had ever breathed it before. To the north was the towering 8400-foot-high volcano we had just flown over. It was eight miles away, but because of its enormity it seemed much closer. To the south was the immense marine-blue Pacific Ocean disappearing into eternity. A chain of islands was visible along the horizon—the largest being Kodiak, home of the biggest grizzly bears on earth. We watched mammoth whales as they swam and spouted in the icy waters between our camp and the islands. Across the bay to the east was a mountain range where a volcano had erupted ages ago, leaving a rusty-ore and golden-sulfur-stained caldron silhouetted against the brilliant white snowcaps. Suddenly from around the rocky shoreline below flew a bald eagle, landing on the beach just below us. I could hardly believe my eyes! His brilliant head covered with white feathers glowed in the sun like a kingly crown. He sat majestically near the water and seemed to enjoy the warmth of the sun's rays. He was the first of many eagles we would see in their native habitat.

Our camp was a sight to behold. It belongs to my friends J.W. and Dawn Smith, who have guided fishermen in Alaska for many years, primarily during the few weeks every summer when the weather is tolerable and the quality of fishing is unsurpassed. They lease the land from the state and have a wonderful facility. All the supplies are stored in a bear-proof cache built of logs that had drifted up on the shoreline over the years. (There are no trees large enough in the area to provide such a shelter.) Every log was hand-carried from the coastline where they had washed up from faraway places. Fresh water was tapped-in from a spring on the hillside just above us for cooking, drinking, and bathing. Small propane bottles were flown in to service the cook stoves in the kitchen tent and hot showers. Thankfully, there were no telephones or electricity, but I must admit the hot water and delicious home-cooked meals made the Alaska wilderness even more heavenly.

That afternoon, after everyone was settled in, the lure of the salmon called. We trekked down the hill decked in waders, vests, and raincoats, rods in hand, ready to sample some of that famously good fishing. The temperatures in mid-July are mild, but it can get very windy, sometimes blowing up to 50 miles per hour, which makes controlling a fly rod's line somewhat challenging. Occasional light to very heavy rain can occur almost any time of day, and the waters in the bay, rivers, and streams are very cold as a result of melting snow and glaciers. Proper gear is a necessity. Along with all the standard equipment, I packed two or more cameras at all times. I was carrying quite a load. That afternoon we stayed in the immediate area below camp, but on subsequent days my friend Rusty and I became more adventuresome, hiking several miles a day. I wanted to leave no stone of this wilderness area unturned.

As we followed bear tracks along the shoreline toward our fishing spot, I noticed the tide was beginning to enter the bay and fill the lowest areas of the riverbed. It was shortly thereafter that the salmon made their way from the ocean into the shallow waters of the bay. They were swimming upstream to the rivers at the base of the northern hills to spawn. It wasn't long before the bay was full of water and migrating salmon. It was time to fish!

We were hoping to catch any of the five varieties of Pacific salmon that afternoon: reds (sockeye), pinks, king (Chinook), chums, and silvers (coho), and maybe some Dolly Varden trout. It wasn't long before "Got him!" and "There he is!" echoed from the rising waters. What a fight the fish put up, especially on fly rods. Tips bent toward the water like candlesticks in the hot sun. It took anywhere from 10 to 20 minutes to land a fish, especially the big chums and kings. What a great couple of hours it was! We caught fish with almost every cast.

Most of the fish we caught that week were released so they could continue their swim upstream to complete their life cycle, but we kept a few for some very special meals.

After fishing, we trudged through the water to a large rock outcropping near the shoreline for a better vantage point. As we were observing the salmon below the surface, we heard a strange noise behind us coming from deep within the fallen rocks. In a few moments, a female sea otter emerged with five young ones. It appeared we were intruding on the privacy of their home,

> To go fishing is the chance to wash one's soul with pure air, with the rush of the brook, or with the shimmer of sun on blue water.
>
> HERBERT HOOVER

about five feet from where we were sitting. They scurried off into the cold water of the bay and proceeded to swim and play as if they were putting on a show for us. The six fuzzy little creatures carried on with their routine undaunted by our curiosity until we went back up the hill for dinner.

After a wonderfully relaxing dinner, and before we retired to our tents, J.W. discussed the agenda for the next few days. The last thing on his list was bears. He verified a fact I had already surmised—we were camped in their backyard. Every precaution was taken not to attract them. All food scraps were disposed of in the bay each evening, and other trash was burned. If anyone heard or saw a bear in camp at night, we were to scream "Bear!" at the top of our lungs to alert everyone else. We were assured the bears were as scared of us as we were of them, and they would spook away from loud noises. But for everyone's safety, every precaution must be observed.

J.W. related a story of how a bear stuck its head inside his tent one night. He said he was so startled that he reached out and punched it in the nose. That sent the bear running. Knowing J.W. the way I do, he's just fearless enough to do something like that. I preferred the alternative method, which is to stand in groups of three or more, scream loudly, and wave our arms. I'd rather not chance leaving any body parts in the Alaskan wilderness as a souvenir for some big bear to brag about. As a last resort, the guides were armed with shotguns filled with pepper spray and buckshot designed specifically not to kill the bears but to scare them away. This technique would be demonstrated more than once out of necessity before our adventure would end.

Brown bears are huge animals. Adult females this time of year averaged 400 to 500 pounds. Males ranged from 500 to 900 pounds, with some giants reaching 1200 pounds or more. They are massive animals that can run at speeds up to 40 miles per hour. They can catch a horse in a short distance, so you can take it to the bank that you won't outrun one! Many are more than nine feet tall when they stand on their hind legs. That week I personally watched several large bears stand up when they caught our scent or when they were searching for salmon in the water. They are very intimidating creatures with their extremely large teeth and sharp claws.

When the "bear briefing" concluded, I headed off to my cozy sleeping bag around nine thirty for a good night's rest before our first full day of fishing. It was at least three hours before I was able to doze off, partly due to the fact it was still light outside, but primarily because my eyes and ears were on high alert for bears and other wild critters. I took a few minutes to make some journal entries and then just laid back and listened to the sounds of the wilderness. I heard the cries of seagulls feeding along the shoreline and an occasional wolf howl in the distance. The waves from the Pacific Ocean crashing on the rocky coastline finally sang me to sleep. I awoke the next morning, most thankfully, with the rising sun and all of my limbs still attached.

Just Another Day in Paradise

The same bright sun I dozed off with the night before woke me the following morning. I'd completely missed the dark of night because of its brief appearance that time of year. As I peered out over the pristine terrain from the door of the tent, I felt completely engulfed in something far greater than me. I was alone in the wilderness with no outside pressures or distractions. I can only describe the sensation as the overwhelming presence of the Lord in the beauty of His unspoiled creation.

As I searched for a way to explain my emotions, I discovered that David's words from the book of Psalms best described what I was experiencing:

> You have searched me, Lord,
>   and you know me.
> You know when I sit and when I rise;
>   you perceive my thoughts from afar.
> You discern my going out and my lying down;
>   you are familiar with all my ways.
> Before a word is on my tongue
>   you, Lord, know it completely.
> You hem me in behind and before,
>   and you lay your hand upon me.
> Such knowledge is too wonderful for me,
>   too lofty for me to attain.

Where can I go from your Spirit?
>   Where can I flee from your presence?
If I go up to the heavens, you are there;
>   if I make my bed in the depths, you are there.
If I rise on the wings of the dawn,
>   if I settle on the far side of the sea,
even there your hand will guide me,
>   your right hand will hold me fast.
If I say, "Surely the darkness will hide me
>   and the light become night around me,"
even the darkness will not be dark to you;
>   the night will shine like the day,
>   for darkness is as light to you
>   (Psalm 139:1-12).

After several moments of contemplation, I was interrupted by the aroma of hot coffee floating up the hill. That was followed by the tantalizing smell of frying bacon. I quickly arose, dressed, and descended to the cook tent to begin another day in the great outdoors. After a great breakfast, we packed our lunches, grabbed our gear, and trekked down the slippery hillside for a full day of fishing.

We were blessed to have Russ and Rich, two tireless and talented young guides who shared their time between our group and the other guests. They were willing to venture wherever we wanted to go and were always nearby for protection and assistance, which we needed on more than one occasion. Several times I found a fly hook deeply imbedded into my neck, backside, or vest while trying to hurl it out in the gusting wind. I'm sure they enjoyed a few laughs at the end of the day at this rookie's expense. There were also a few occasions when a big grizzly decided not to spook despite our waving and yelling. A little more encouragement to skedaddle from the shotguns always did the trick.

Our group hiked four miles north of camp, about halfway to the base of the volcano. We fished the river all the way up the bay and then followed another stream back southward toward the ocean. We ended up on the opposite side of the bay from camp. Everyone had caught a lot of nice fish by noon. The numbers varied depending on who was telling the story.

We had romped through the heart of bear country and never had an encounter. There were many tracks on the east side of camp, but we saw no actual bears. Later we climbed up a giant sand dune for a better vantage point to relax and have lunch. Camp was visible about a mile or so away. The Pacific was directly over the dune behind us, and to our right was a large meadow with lush, deep grass. As we enjoyed our sandwiches, we noticed a large tan bear and two cubs moving through the meadow a few hundred yards away. We'd been warned about the dangers of females with cubs. Their maternal instinct to protect their offspring could cause them to attack if they sensed danger. As the bears got closer, we found ourselves sitting up and paying more attention. It was a good opportunity for photographs. We might not get this close again all week, so I shot away. Little did I know what was to come! Within a few minutes, the bears were about 100 yards away. This was as close as we had been to bears since we arrived. We were downwind, so she didn't see or smell us until she got to the river just below the dune where we were perched. Russ thought that was too close for comfort, so we all stood up together, waving and yelling. She stood up on her hind legs and pawed the air in our direction, the cubs hiding behind her in the grass. She soon turned and moved away, heading up river for a more peaceful place to fish. *That was easy!* I thought.

After lunch we walked down the Pacific side of the dune to see if fish were biting in the ocean breakers. We waded out about 50 yards before the water got deep. The wind was blowing hard and the waves hit us with ice-cold spray. Some seals were swimming a few yards in front of us, probably catching fish for lunch. They were difficult to keep in sight because of the breaking waves and the wind-blown spray. From time to time one would raise its head out of the water. I could see its big eyes looking curiously in our direction. Then like lightning, one swam in front of me at blazing speed and charged Rusty, nipping at his leg as it passed by. We took that as a sign we were trespassing and headed for dry land.

We proceeded along the shoreline to the mouth of the bay, directly across from the steep hill where our camp was located. The banks of the hill we were currently on were very steep with long, clawlike fingers of volcanic rock extending into the ocean. They curved on around the coastline as far as we could see. As we investigated these odd outcroppings, we found other volcanic rocks had fallen from the rocky cliffs above and were lodged between the crevasses among a myriad of clam and mussel shells. There were millions of them stacked on top of and beside each other as far as the eye could see.

What I found especially interesting was the shape of the rocks. They must have been there for centuries. The rocks on the cliffs were mostly square and rectangular chunks of volcanic stone, but these rocks of various sizes were almost all perfectly round. When a wave rolled in and covered the spires, all the rocks trapped in the crevasses were rolled backward, then tumbled forward as the water receded. Years, even centuries, of being washed in the waves of the ocean had smoothed the once rough and brittle edges into perfect circles. I was reminded of God's principle of how the washing of His Word produces perfection in our lives and smooths our rough edges.

That evening after dinner, standing on the side of the cliff and looking down toward the outcroppings we'd explored earlier, I spotted a bull moose on the beach with his mate. They were contently grazing on some vitamin-rich kelp that had washed ashore. The moose weren't nearly as impressed with the rocks as I was. In fact, the rocks made their navigation of the coastline much more difficult and were a nuisance to them. But what did they care? I decided. After all, they had each other, a beautiful place to live, and a protein-rich dinner to satisfy their needs. They couldn't be more content! It was just the close of another routine day for them in the great outdoors.

25

Too Close for Comfort

On a bright, sunny morning, Rusty, our guide Rich, and I hiked to the upper river near a mountain called Homer Hill, just south of the volcano. Fishing along the way, we caught pinks and chums with almost every cast. Suddenly Rusty spotted a large eagle's nest in a tree beside the rocky cliff above. He stopped just beneath it for photographs. The female was perched on a limb above the nest basking in the warm sun as the heads of the young eaglets poked up and peered out from their lofty home.

We proceeded down the river, stopping on a gravel bed in a narrow fork to fish both sides. Always cognizant of our proximity to bears, I observed what I thought was a bear about 300 yards west of us. We were deep in bear territory, and alder trees were very thick on the hillside above the bank. I yelled "Bear!" to warn the others. We were accustomed to seeing several bears by now, but we were still very cautious, making a lot of noise as we walked. What I thought was a bear turned out to be a large caribou grazing behind some alder trees beside the river. I couldn't see its head behind the brush. When he moved in our direction, we sat down in the gravel and became very still. He walked within 20 yards of where we were seated. He was a magnificent creature—a large stag with a huge rack just beginning to shed the velvet from the towering antlers. He was as curious as we were and pranced around for several minutes, grazing in the lush grass along the shore and casually observing us as he looked up between bites. We took this opportunity to take several photos. As we slowly stood up, he turned and trotted a few steps away, moving closer to the brushy hillside but still staying pretty close to us.

It was beginning to mist, so we put our cameras safely away in our backpacks and resumed our quest for salmon, keeping an eye on the caribou from time to time. The peaceful sounds of the rippling river were suddenly interrupted by the loud shatter of cracking tree limbs. The caribou flinched and jerked his head up from the grass, looking into the brush on the hillside. In a fraction of a second, a huge grizzly leaped from the thicket in an attempt to catch the caribou. The hunter's eyes were fixed like radar on the big buck. Hungry and meaning business, he let out a vicious growl, exposing his huge teeth. The three of us froze like stones on that gravel bed. All we could move was our eyes as we watched the ensuing chase.

The massive bear pounded through the water as he pursued the caribou across several divisions in the river, snarling loudly all the way. The caribou had a decisive lead and escaped in the flat just south of the volcano, where he had been grazing moments before. I couldn't believe my eyes! None of us could. It was by far the largest bear we'd seen all week and certainly the closest we had been to one. Not one of us got a picture of the event! It never even entered our minds until the entire incident was over. We had missed photographs of a lifetime, but thankfully we'd also escaped with a memory we will never forget. When both animals were out of sight, we sat down on the gravel bar in dead silence, taking in what we'd seen and how close we'd been to a hunting bear.

When we could finally feel our hearts beating again, we went back to fishing. I looked up to watch a male eagle on his approach to the family in the nest. He was probably the mate to the female and had a magnificent wingspan of seven or eight feet. He circled three times about 50 feet above and then dove close enough for photos. My camera was around my neck. I'd learned my lesson—rain or not, it was not going in the pack.

Once again we spotted the frustrated bear along the river, in about the same spot where I'd first seen the caribou. Assuming our frozen positions, we made certain this time to have our cameras ready. He continued following the river, coming directly toward us. When he was about 100 yards away, Rich wasted no time getting his shotgun in the ready position. All we could do was stand there and hope he would turn away. But he kept coming. He was now on the bank of the river about 30 yards away. We jumped up, waving and yelling, but he didn't turn away. He was mad, I figured. He'd lost the caribou and was hungry and very frustrated. As we continued to wave and yell, he stood up on his hind legs and shook his head from side to side, growling and pawing. I managed to snap some great photographs of the massive carnivore as he continued his angry display for several minutes. He finally turned and lumbered off in search of salmon. When he disappeared out of sight, we decided that was enough

> The sportsman lives his life vicariously—for he secretly yearns to have lived before, in a simpler time.
> A time when his love for the land, water, fish and wildlife would be more than just part of his life—it would be his state of mind.
>
> JIM SLINSKY

action for one day. We made the long hike back to camp to share our amazing stories with our comrades. This was one fishing story they surely couldn't top!

That evening after dinner we sat on the windy cliff above the bay and watched several bears as they fished for salmon. It is an incredible sight to see these huge, clumsy-looking creatures calmly stalk a fish from the shore, charge into the icy water, and in the blink of an eye retrieve one. Salmon provide most of the diet necessary for hibernation. This time of year, bears consume 80 to 90 pounds of food daily to gain 3 or 4 pounds of fat. During the summer salmon runs, they will gain several hundred pounds to sustain them through months of hibernation. As I pondered this fact, I thought how the three of us on the gravel bar would have been enough food to last a bear almost a week.

Another exciting adventure drew to a close as the sunlight cast long shadows across the bay. After all the bear and fish stories of the day had been shared, one of the older gentlemen in camp stood up, stared across the expansive panorama, and commented, "How insignificant we humans are when compared to the vastness of earth."

It was easy to feel insignificant in comparison to this overwhelming landscape of 8000-foot mountains and giant grizzlies. Though dwarfed by the magnitude of the land and amazed by the potentially danger-ous wildlife, I was comfortable and at peace. Admittedly, I think I still slept with one eye open.

·26·

The Ride of a Lifetime

Equally exciting as the bear and caribou encounter was the helicopter ride to an adjacent bay the following day. The experience was exhilarating. The sights were incredible as we flew from over the mountains, exploring areas that were unreachable by any other means of transportation. Our early morning flight took us over the snow-capped cauldron of an ancient volcano. A herd of caribou was pawing through the thin layer of snow to nip at tender new shoots of grass. As we glided and turned, soaring at great speeds on the powerful wind currents of the Pacific, we were able to see for miles in all directions.

After crossing the mountain, we swooped down into a lush valley where several bears were grazing with cubs by their sides. Many looked up in amazement, standing on their hind legs and pawing as though they wanted to knock us out of the sky. We observed a number of eagles that were similarly startled by the roar of the helicopter. They rose from their nests and flew away.

We ascended another mountain and caught our first glimpse of the next bay. A dense fog covered everything and, for a moment, we were engulfed. As we descended to 50 feet above the water surface, we regained visibility. The pilot set the chopper down on the beach. Four of us got off and quickly gathered our gear for a day of fishing. As soon as we were clear, the pilot signaled and took off. He would return for us in six hours.

It was dark and dreary with a heavy mist in the air from the thick fog. The shoreline was completely covered with bear tracks of all sizes. The bay was narrow, and several rivers fed into it from the mountains just north of us. Large rock pinnacles blanketed in mist stood like sentinels jutting against the backdrop of the barely visible Pacific Ocean.

Across a nearby meadow, I spotted a large female bear with two cubs walking away from us. Thankfully, the helicopter had probably spooked her into moving the opposite direction from us. Three of the guys decided to fish the river just beyond the shore where we'd landed. I chose to video the area while it wasn't raining.

As I zoomed in on the top of one pinnacle, I discovered a large eagle's nest. A female sat on the rocks just above, and I could distinguish the heads of several eaglets peering from their lofty home. After several minutes of walking with the viewfinder to my eye, I realized I was standing almost directly beneath the pinnacle. Just as I began to lower the camera, the female swooped down in my direction. I flinched and ducked as she flew past. I'd obviously infringed on her territory, and she was not a happy mother.

Bald eagles have superb eyesight that enables them to spot fish from high in the air and then dive, folding their giant seven- to eight-foot wingspans to reach speeds approaching 100 miles per hour. Their powerful talons can strike with twice the force of a rifle bullet.

I quickly retreated, and she returned to her perch just above the nest. I walked along the shore, frequently looking over my shoulder to make sure the protective mom remained on the rock. Sitting at the very top of a nearby pinnacle and partially camouflaged by the fog was a large male eagle, certain to be the mate of the one I'd just encountered.

As I videoed him, the female rose from her perch and flew to join him on top of the slender stone. The two beautiful birds sat breast to breast and looked at each other. After a few moments, they touched their beaks together in what appeared to be a kiss. The male immediately flew out over the ocean and disappeared in the fog. I gathered the female had placed her order for lunch, and he went out to pick it up! I sat on the beach for 15 minutes and watched as she returned to her eaglets. After about a half hour, the male returned with a fish. Everyone in the nest enjoyed a nice meal together. Both genders are famously good parents and often alternate sitting on the nest and caring for their young. I was so thankful for the up-close-and-personal observation.

While I had been eagle watching, the guys were catching salmon with every cast. The fish were swimming into the bay by the thousands to make their way upstream to spawn. I joined in on the action for a couple of hours until my arms got so tired from fighting fish that I decided to do more exploring.

I persuaded our guide, Russ, to take me to a large waterfall a couple of miles upriver so I could get some pictures. He was happy to accommodate me, and the two of us set out along the river, stopping occasionally to observe the large numbers of salmon. Some of the fish had arrived at their destination and were preparing their nests in the gravel near the banks of the river. The water was crystal clear. It was amazing to watch them dig holes with their tails and arrange the rocks with their snouts. Some nests already contained pink eggs, and the salmon hovered over them in protection mode.

We continued our quest, making a lot of noise to spook away any bears lurking behind the thick brush. As we drew closer to the waterfall, the river current grew much stronger. The determined salmon, anxious to make it to their destination, fought tirelessly against the force of the water. We turned at a bend in the river, and from behind the brush we saw raging water. It was so loud we could barely hear each other. As we got closer, no bears were awaiting us, but salmon were jumping, trying to reach

the top of the waterfall. The homing instinct and the determination of these fish are truly two of life's great miracles. It was a stunning sight as icy water poured through the narrow, fog-filled canyon to fall several feet into a clear pool filled with colorful fish.

We sat down on a gravel bed and removed some of our gear to

lighten the load. I photographed while Russ climbed a steep rock cliff to reach the top of the waterfall. I would have joined him—if nothing else just to prove that a 50-year-old guy could keep up with a 20-something, strapping young man, but unfortunately because we were on a tight schedule and couldn't afford to miss our afternoon flight out I wanted to take as many pictures as possible.

After a while, we hiked back and joined the other fishermen at the coast a few minutes before the chopper arrived. By now the fog was too heavy to fly back over the hills, so we flew along the coastline, just above the water until we reached our bay. When we turned the corner leading into our inlet, the sun was shining and it was a clear, beautiful view. No fog! My senses were completely overloaded with the drastic weather changes, the dramatic views from the helicopter, and the studious observation of eagles, bears, and fish.

The Cycle of Life

The most fascinating truth I learned from my week in the Alaskan wilderness was taught by the salmon. Swimming with all their might, jumping headfirst into roaring waterfalls, and fighting swift currents, they seek the exact location of their birth to give life to a new generation. They are a perfect example of fulfilling their calling.

The life cycle of the Pacific salmon begins after the male and female make a perilous journey upstream from the sea and undergo a physical transformation that prepares them for reproduction, which is known as spawning. Salmon are anadromous fish, meaning they hatch in fresh water, migrate to the sea (salt water), and then return to the fresh water where they originated to breed. Some varieties stay in fresh water from one to three years, but most stay only a few months.

Salmon spend up to seven years in the food-rich ocean. They grow rapidly from the available nutrients. They have a strong homing instinct that drives them back to their fresh-water birth streams to spawn. It is fascinating how each succeeding generation of the salmon population returns to the same spawning grounds. They locate their birth streams through their sense of smell. It is mind-boggling that they can leave a remote, fresh-water stream, swim in the vastness of the Pacific Ocean, and then return years later to the exact spot of their births.

As the predominantly silver-colored salmon enter the stream, a transformation takes place. The silver changes to vibrant hues of reds, purples, and greens. These bright colors allow the different species to identify their mates during spawning. During this transformation in the fresh water, the adult fish don't feed, so their physical condition deteriorates.

Once the female salmon reaches her chosen spawning ground, she digs in the gravel of the stream with her tail and snout to form a nest. This activity attracts the males, who defend their breeding rights by swimming into and biting each other. The dominant male swims alongside the female and fertilizes the eggs as they fall into the nest. The female may release several batches of eggs over a period of a few days. After they are fertilized, she covers them with gravel for protection and defends them for about a week. Then both male and female die.

In a few days, inch-long salmon emerge from their eggs. They receive life-sustaining nourishment and oxygen from a tiny yolk sac attached to their abdomens. Once they lose their yolk sacs and mature into fingerlings, their color changes and they blend into the gravel, thus camouflaging them from predators. They are now large enough to rely on small aquatic insects for food. Some varieties remain in fresh water for a year or more, while others move almost immediately to the salt water of the Pacific. Before migrating downstream to the ocean, the young salmon go through a process called smoltification, which completes their transition from fresh water fish to saltwater fish.

During their life in the ocean, some varieties travel thousands of miles. They feed off plankton, crustaceans, and other small fish while growing rapidly. Then they return to their ancestral spawning grounds, and the cycle repeats.

After the adult salmon die, their decomposing bodies provide food for bears, birds, and predators. The carcasses also provide rich nutrients for the soil.

An interesting analogy can be drawn from the life cycle of the salmon. First, they function exactly like God designed them to. After their birth, they remain close to their nest while feeding from a yolk sac, much the same way humans receive the necessary life-giving nutrients from their mothers' milk. New Christians receive "milk"— simple truths of the gospel they learn from Christians and God's Word.

As salmon mature in size, the young fish venture out of their nest, exploring new territory and learning to catch food. Humans follow much the same order. Infants move from crawling to walking, and graduate from milk to feeding themselves softer foods and meat. As young Christians mature, they move from the milk of God's Word to exploring the real meat—learning to read, study, and apply deeper biblical principles to become more like Christ.

When the salmon are mature enough, they swim into the vast ocean to grow and enjoy the freedom and fullness of life the sea has to offer. When humans are physically mature enough, they leave the security of their families and venture out into the vast world to make lives of their own, discovering many opportunities that await them. When the young Christian reaches maturity, he or she ventures out into this world enjoying the freedom of the gospel and sharing the good news of Jesus with others.

God, in His perfect love, has chosen to share His creation and its wonderful cycle of life with us. We can learn a lesson from the salmon.

> My heart, the sun hath set.
> Night's paths with dews are wet.
> Sleep comes without regret;
> Stars rise when sun is set.
> All's well. God loves thee yet,
> Heart, smile, sleep sweet, not fret.
>
> WILLIAM QUAYLE

Live life to the fullest! Never take it for granted. Life is a gift from God to be enjoyed, nurtured, conserved, and shared. Never view yourself as an insignificant part of God's grand creation. The determined salmon and mighty bear are satisfied to live and die in the wilderness, fulfilling their purpose on earth. But we humans have the wonderful option of living on this earth while glorifying our heavenly Father and looking forward to spending eternity with Him.

While we can often be overwhelmed by the magnificence and beauty of creation all around us, we need to remember that God loved us more than any other part of His creation. He sent His Son to walk among our kind, sharing stories about a place called heaven—a place more beautiful than anything we've ever seen. In fact, it's far greater than anything we can experience in the great outdoors. And through Jesus, we have an invitation to live for eternity in heaven with Him! We are indeed wonderfully blessed.

Part 4

EVERYBODY NEEDS A HERO

The Great American Cowboy

Many years have passed now since I wrote my first short stories about my family's life as pioneers in Texas. I grew up dreaming of being a cowboy riding by my granddad's side. Pushin' cows to Kansas across prairies and through rivers in the rain, under sunny skies, and amid droughts. Sleeping under the stars and singing the cattle into a peaceful calm as the lazy moon slowly rises in the east. Even though my grandfather passed away when I was very young, I knew a great deal about his life and times, and I somehow whittled out a dream from his stories and experiences that was uniquely my own.

It was a dream well-conceived and greatly fulfilling. It was based on heroes who worked honestly and endlessly in the land the Lord provided. It included people who were good parents and good stewards of the land. Folks raising families, along with the food to fill their hungry children, friends, and strangers when times were hard and jobs were scarce in the Great Depression and Dust Bowl years that stole livestock and livelihoods. Pioneers were thankful for their gifts and talents and realized the importance of hard work and sharing what they had. Caring for friends and neighbors was as natural as caring for their own families.

I'm the first to admit my art and writing are pleasurable ways to share a portion of the bravado and great history my family has experienced settling the Old West and creating the new one. Such a wonderful heritage!

It is only now, with a fabulous wife the Lord placed so very lovingly by my side, after years as a successful artist, and as a man loved greatly by my wonderful children and terrific grandchildren that I'm beginning to fully realize how truly special my heritage is. My hope lies within something from the past, something from the present, and the joy of knowing my relationship with Jesus Christ guarantees my celebration with Him for my future and eternity.

Right now I'm in a chapter in life where heroes are needed. And not just for the young ones being raised up, but for me too. I need to draw from the strengths of the ones I loved and admired so I can believe in hope for our nation and the lost souls of the world. Where are the heroes?

Life isn't easy these days for a lot of folks. As a fifth-generation Texan, I have believed as my family has for generations that our lives will always be okay while we live in this great land. "Work hard and do what is right, and all will be well when you are old" was our motto. My wonderful and always well-intentioned dad says, "You can be anything you want to be—if you work hard enough." I'm sure my granddads are looking down and smiling, occasionally elbowing one another in the ribs and laughing. One might say, "He's just like you, Bill. I knew he was gonna do that." The other will probably reply, "He's a good boy. Just give him some time. He'll see the light eventually." But am I living up to "all I can be" and letting the great Trail Boss direct my steps?

My love for the West and the great American cowboy will never die. It's as big a part of my life and culture as anything I've ever known or loved. I've saved every old saddle, bridle, spur, and other western paraphernalia you can imagine. My studio walls are plastered with more than 250 years of history. But I find it a rare occasion nowadays to don my Stetson unless I'm working a few cows, hunting, or reliving some old western music with my guitar.

Our Western heroes wore their hats like badges of pride and courage. It was one of the most important tools of their trade. The cowboy hat kept the cowpoke dry in the falling rain, warm in the drifting snow, and protected his face from the sultry sun.

In some ways I feel it's disrespectful for drugstore cowboys at the big rodeos or the nearest dance halls to dress up like cowboys and pretend to be part of their culture.

The Hats My Grandfathers Wore

When Granddad was on the trail pushing cows or breaking broncs between cattle drives, his cowboy hat had a five-inch brim with a high crown. The brim was wide enough to cover his face and neck from the blistering sun, and the crown was high enough to draw the rising fire of heat out the few well-placed, pencil-sized holes along its curve. It didn't take a genius to figure out what a person needed to survive the challenges of punching cows. This was in the late 1800s, when the last cattle drives depended on men who could ride, rope, and shoot. As Wild Bill Hickok told it, the cowboy could brave the strongest current to save a lone calf in a flood or deliver an entire herd through the snow to the steakhouse in Dodge City. The cowboy could shoot a silver dollar in the air at 50 paces and break the world's wildest horse in a New York second by just whispering to the little feller. When necessary, he could take down a challenging buffalo or bag a fleeting elk at a hundred yards. For him, this was the great American West's way of life.

People who had insatiable appetites for the cowboy's steak focused on the beef. They didn't care how the cows got to the stockyards or who brought them. While people across the universe still savor the taste of a great steak, they no longer care about the people in charge of delivering it. Society once wanted to know the men behind the availability of beef.

Since there are so few real cowboys left, primarily because they can't afford to pay the taxes on their ranches, much less feed a family or put a child through college, the dream is dying. As Wild Bill said in 1883, "If we can't make a living at it, let's make it a show." And he did! He ran the world-famous Wild West Show for years. It was based on the cowboy way of life, but was far from the reality of the day-in and day-out honor, courage, and respectful way cowboys lived.

Have you noticed that cowboy hats became bigger and rodeos more numerous as the traditional Old West way of life faded into the distant past? My grandfathers, who were the true cattlemen of the real "good ol' days" bought smaller hats as they grew older. Eventually, they didn't need their hats for protection because they no longer worked in the sun chasing cows. They wore them along with their boots, sometimes with pant legs tucked in as if in working mode, when headed to the coffee shop to chew a little fat with the boys. These gentlemen knew from whence they came, where they were at that day, and where they were going in the future because of their great faith.

> Do what you can, with what you have, where you are.
>
> THEODORE ROOSEVELT

It's been well over 50 years since I've spoken to either of these great gentlemen. My granddads were my heroes, and when they spoke, their thoughts and words changed lives. It's not the size of the hat we wear that proves who we are and what is in our hearts. Rather, it's how we impact others with our lives. While most of the traditional cowboys are gone now, we still see a lot of folks sporting cowboy hats and boots. Seems a lot of people want to be heroes.

Growing Older

I was born with a wild and adventurous heart, always seeking to swing from a vine like Tarzan or chase the bad guys through the canyons with my pistols while riding alongside Roy Rogers and Trigger. I wanted nothing more at that early age than to sit in front of the non-HD, black-and-white, mono-sound television and chase the outlaws at breakneck speed with the Lone Ranger and Gene Autry. They were heroes who stood for respect and courage and always defended the underdogs. They were the white-hat guys who stood for truth, justice, and, as Superman so bravely stated, "the American way." As a child, it was easy to find heroes. Those of us who grew up watching those old television giants are now old enough to have to answer questions asked by our children and grandchildren—but mostly ourselves. Where are the heroes today? Who are they, and how do we find them? What is a "real" hero supposed to look like?

It was quite sobering to wake up one day and realize I was a husband, dad, and even a granddad. Younger folks are looking for guidance and stability. Is it time for me to step up and become a hero for them? I've spent my entire life trying to live the American dream driven by the concepts "Be the very best you can be" and "You can do anything if you just put your mind to it." I've been given many wonderful talents and have enjoyed success in my business. I've seen many beautiful places and shaken the hands of so many great people. But as my brother so tauntingly reminds me from time to time, I am the classic overachiever. I'm a person who takes everything in life so very seriously that there is little or no chance for failure. I will either make it happen or fix it if it is broken. For decades that's been the path I've chosen.

The only problem is that lifestyle rarely if ever improves anyone's life. In fact, it often has the opposite effect—draining energy, joy, and peace from the person and everyone around him or her. I was in need of a helper, but I didn't know it. It is one thing to do a job to the best of your ability, but it's quite another when the pursuit of your dreams leaves little time for making friends and nourishing relationships. My life was out of balance.

One evening I was sitting outdoors around sundown, just enjoying a gentle breeze, when I was transported in my mind back some 45 years to my grandparents' backyard. I could see us all sitting in the chairs on the back porch at dusk feeling the soft wind and appreciating the cadences generated from the cicadas nesting in the giant mesquite trees. Few words were spoken. Some folks whistled, some rocked, but most just sat and peered peacefully into twilight until it was time to go in for supper. It was a time to rest and reflect on the day and the goodness of God.

Granddad and Grandma Terry discovered peace on earth and enjoyed it immensely. They found contentment in their small home despite living through some very difficult years. They never made much money off their crops or livestock. They agonizingly buried two of their three sons. But their faith remained strong and their hearts were focused on trusting God for all things. "Make sure that your character is free from the love of money, being content with what you have: for He Himself has said, 'I will never desert you, nor will I ever forsake you' so that we confidently say, 'The Lord is my Helper, I will not be afraid. What will man do to me?'" (Hebrews 13:5-6). There can be no greater joy than living life every day with the consciousness of knowing the God who has no limitations and no boundaries confining or separating His love for us.

During the past several years, I've discovered how my pushing and controlling of my career and personal life caused the joy and peace in my heart to diminish considerably. I reached a point where I no longer trusted God to keep things together. I felt like I had to do it on my own, yet I knew deep down I couldn't. Life had become overwhelming as I tried to maintain more responsibilities than was humanly possible.

Like so many, I lost confidence in government institutions and programs responsible for ensuring safe retirement. My faith in God was weak.

Although I had sold out to the old proverb that I could be anything I wanted to be so many years ago, I was forced to face the reality that it wasn't true. I'd been a Christian most of my life, but I had chosen to believe and trust in the secular system for operating my business. I confined the death of Jesus to my ability to gain salvation and eternal life and excluded Him from taking the lead in my career. I had a real issue with faith—not fully believing Hebrews 11:6: "Without faith it is impossible to please Him, for he who comes to God must believe that He is and that He is a rewarder of those who seek Him." While I talked a good story about the goodness of the Lord and tried to bring glory to Him in all things, there was part of me that wouldn't let go. I didn't know it, but I needed a Helper. I knew in my heart that I wasn't pleasing God because I had little peace and joy. I had taken my eyes off the prize:

> Storms make trees have deeper roots.
>
> CLAUDE MCDONALD

> Lay aside every encumbrance and the sin which so easily entangles us, and let us run with endurance the race that is set before us, fixing our eyes on Jesus, the author and perfecter of faith, who for the joy set before Him endured the cross, despising the shame, and has sat down at the right hand of the throne of God. For consider Him who has endured such hostility by sinners against Himself, so that you may not grow weary and lose heart (Hebrews 12:1-3).

It's great to know we can fix our eyes on Jesus. Our past is over and our future isn't here yet, so living by faith can only be done in the present. Every day is a new opportunity to grow and turn more of our lives over to Jesus.

Recently while contemplating the recent death of one of my cousins, I was reminded of the necessity of "fixing our eyes on Jesus."

Charlie Mason was a man of very small stature, standing just a bit over five feet and weighing in around 130 pounds in his prime. He grew up a cowboy, was a professional bull rider on the Pro Rodeo Circuit, and belonged to the Professional Rodeo Cowboy Association. He rode with some of the all-time great cowboys, such as Larry Mahan, winner of seven "All Around Cowboy" world titles. I watched Charlie ride bulls on one of the first rodeo performances broadcast on live television in the early 1950s. Charlie was, as we Texans put it, "as tough as a boot." What he lacked in size, he made up in endurance and faith.

He was 16 years my elder, so he was more like an uncle than a cousin. I admired him greatly and asked a few years back how he managed to stay on those bulls so long. He cocked his Stetson-clad head to the right and looked up at me from his wheelchair. He said there was only one way he could do it. "Never take your eyes off the bull's eyes. If you do, you will end up flat on your back every time."

To know which way the animal is going to turn and spin so they can adjust their position to stay on, riders must watch the bull's eyes. Charlie had faith to ride under seemingly impossible conditions. He was supposedly way too small to rodeo successfully, but he knew the importance of keeping his eyes on the prize. He rode with great confidence and faith, and he was a great inspiration to many. He also shared with me the times he had to just let go of the rope because he didn't have the strength that day to make the 8-second ride. There was no future in holding on to a ride headed toward disaster and probable pain and injury. "Sometimes it's best just to let go," he told me. When I realized my ineffectiveness in controlling and fixing my life, much less help anyone else, I knew it was time to let go. I finally was realizing I needed a Helper.

Letting Go

Call me hardheaded or just plain stubborn, but for many years I believed I was living a pretty good life as a Christian, an artist, and a businessman who was raised by godly parents who experienced many difficult days yet held firmly to their faith. They made sure my brother and I grew up with great educations, including music and art lessons. We were also in church three times a week. My brother and I believed in God and the American dream of being all we could be.

It took several decades of doing what I thought was right in the sight of God to finally realize I'd taken my eyes off Jesus so things weren't going as they should. He had specifically designed a very special life for me, but because I was trying to control everything, I felt empty and frustrated. I couldn't get a handle around Galatians 2:20, which I had once known so well: "I have been crucified with Christ; and it is no longer I who live, but Christ lives in me; and the life which I now live in the flesh I live by faith in the Son of God, who loved me and gave Himself up for me."

I can't tell you how many times I heard the phrase "Let go and let God." There is nothing more frustrating for an overachiever than to be told to let someone else handle whatever is going on—even if it is God promoting the thought. I was trying to be a hero by being in charge of everything. How can a bull rider let go of the rope and expect to stay on the bull for 8 seconds? How can a barrel racer drop the reins and still expect her horse to circle all the barrels at the fastest possible speed? It's impossible, right?

One Sunday our church was visited by three missionaries and their wives, whom we supported in the interior of Mexico. After the service, our minister asked if I would help him entertain the group over lunch since I knew a bit of Spanish and they spoke very little English. I volunteered, remembering I'd only put a small roast in the oven before church services. I ended up with 10 people for lunch! When I raised the lid on the roast before lunch, it was barely enough for four people. I opened canned goods and threw some rolls in the oven. I sliced the roast razor thin.

Time to say grace came. I was embarrassed to host a meal when I had such small portions for so many to share, but I prayed with thanksgiving and asked God to multiply our meal to meet our needs. Everyone filled their plates buffet-style, and as I brought up the rear to fill my plate, I saw that there were only two razor thin slices of roast left. Some of the ladies had declined to serve themselves any roast, probably out of respect for me.

I joined the group at the table, and we communicated as best we could with my broken Spanish. I could see the men were quite hungry and had almost emptied their plates by the time I got to my seat at the dining table. Wishing to be a good host, I motioned for them to go back for more. I recall saying rather flippantly, "Poquito mas amigos?" (A little more, my friends?) As I made my way to the kitchen, I sensed God had something more in mind.

When I opened the lid to the roast I gasped—not a full-blown scream out loud, but it sure was a loud one in my mind. I'd never seen anything like this before. The entire dish was filled with meat, sliced thinly as I had done previously. I looked at my preacher as the men loaded their plates again and said something like, "Wow! It's completely full!" Our Mexican friends knew enough English to laugh and say without surprise, "Oh, it is okay. God does this all the time where we come from."

Their faith showed me that my simple prayer to multiply the meal was my decision to believe God could and would do what He promised. I had responded to an opportunity to meet a need that the Lord placed before me, and He provided the bountiful food. Granted, I prayed more from embarrassment than from faith, but graciously the Lord taught me a huge lesson:

Faith is the assurance of things hoped for, the conviction of things not seen. For by it the men of old gained approval. By faith we understand that the worlds were prepared by the word of God, so that what is seen was not made out of things which are visible (Hebrews 11:1-3).

It was inherently clear to me at that point that I was not the hero. But I also learned that because of my faith, God would supply people's needs when I could not. I had to let go to see what God would do!

Jesus then said to them, "Truly, truly, I say to you, it is not Moses who has given you the bread out of heaven, but it is My Father who gives you the true bread out of heaven. For the bread of God is that which comes down out of heaven, and gives life to the world."

Then they said to Him, "Lord, always give us this bread."

Jesus said to them, "I am the bread of life; he who comes to Me will not hunger, and he who believes in Me will never thirst. But I said to you that you have seen Me, and yet do not believe. All that the Father gives Me will come to Me, and the one who comes to Me I will certainly not cast out. For I have come down from heaven, not to do My own will, but the will of Him who sent Me. This is the will of Him who sent Me, that of all that He has given Me I lose nothing, but raise it up on the last day. For this is the will of My Father, that everyone who beholds the Son and believes in Him will have eternal life, and I Myself will raise him up on the last day" (John 6:32-40).

When we let go and trust Jesus and what He says, He will be our bread and water. He will save us and raise us up. He is our Hero sent from on high! We are able to experience far more of God's goodness through Him than we can ever achieve on our own.

I look back at my life and oftentimes have to scratch my head as I recollect my ignorance and stubbornness. With all the promises of

God I had hidden in my heart, I still acted like a maverick Texas cow. What do I mean by that?

I've been on roundups to push cattle out of the mountains before winter sets in so they will have ample feed through the cold months. I will never forget one year as the sun was setting on a 250,000-acre pasture. I was trying to get back to camp with a dozen or so strays before dark. I was hot and tired from riding up and down the rocky mesas all day, and I was thankful I was nearly done. One particular cow—a maverick of first order—occasionally would sprint away from the bunch and head back into the hills. Four or five times within that last hour on that long autumn day, I would leave the rest of the cows to chase the wild one and drive her back down into the herd. Thankfully, the other cows were so tired, they obediently headed downhill toward the bawling cattle in the catch pens below.

I was reminded of that stubborn maverick when I thought of all those years I believed I could do things my way. No matter how I may have wanted to change, I couldn't produce or force the alterations I needed. I finally realized that my attitude could change from "I can't do this—but You can" if I gave the situations to the Lord. The apostle Paul wrote:

> Do not be conformed to this world, but be transformed by the renewing of your mind, so that you may prove what the will of God is, that which is good and acceptable and perfect. For through the grace given to me I say to everyone among you not to think more highly of himself than he ought to think; but to think so as to have sound judgment, as God has allotted to each a measure of faith (Romans 12:2-3).

When I thought I could do everything on my own and be successful, I was conforming to the world's beliefs. How did that happen? I'd been taught all my life through family, education, and even church that I could be anything and do anything as long as I wanted it badly enough. Now I was finally experiencing a time of change and transformation from the old life of overachieving to becoming a faith-walking,

Holy Spirit-led man of God. No more games, no more control. Philippians 4:6-9 says:

> Be anxious for nothing, but in everything by prayer and supplication with thanksgiving let your requests be made known to God. And the peace of God, which surpasses all comprehension, will guard your hearts and your minds in Christ Jesus. Finally, brethren, whatever is true, whatever is honorable, whatever is right, whatever is pure, whatever is lovely, whatever is of good repute, if there is any excellence and if anything worthy of praise, dwell on these things. The things you have learned and received and heard and seen in me, practice these things, and the God of peace will be with you.

My thinking had to be transformed and my mind had to be renewed *before* I could lose the feelings of anxiousness and desire to control, *before* I could experience true peace. Peace was something I wasn't familiar with. Judging my level of peace according to this Philippians 4 passage, I wasn't doing so well. I wasn't very good at practicing all those great qualities. I needed to experience the simplicity of the Hero who is our bread and water, who is our truth and light. I needed my heart filled with prayers to Him and the assurances of the Holy Spirit. Christ lives in me and wants me to have the faith to allow

Him to control my life. I don't have to take control and make decisions on my own. I don't have to supply all the answers. Jesus has a better way!

And when Jesus returned to heaven to sit at the right hand of the Father, He sent a Helper to abide in us and guide us in God's truths. I needed—and still need—that Helper. "I tell you the truth, it is to your advantage that I go away; for if I do not go away, the Helper will not come to you; but if I go, I will send Him to you" (John 16:7).

Bring On the Help

I am confident of this very thing, that He who began a good work in you will perfect it until the day of Christ Jesus" (Philippians 1:6). Being an independent man for so many years, change didn't come easily. God began His good work in my life many years ago when I accepted Jesus into my heart. The "perfection" of His work has taken many years to progress, and it continues today.

My interest in art began early. I started drawing when I was around three. I wasn't all that great, but my work showed enough potential that at age seven my parents enrolled me in art lessons. With each lesson, my skill improved. It wasn't long until I won awards at local art events. In college, I exhibited my paintings in a major art gallery and pursued a career in art. Western scenes were my favorites then—and remain so because of my family's participation in living in the Old West.

Horses are particularly difficult animals to draw, and drawing people's faces and bodies have always been a challenge for most artists. The first horse I did as a teenager looked like a giraffe, and it garnered several laughs from my friends. A few years later, in a one-man exhibition, an old cowboy studied one of my paintings for several minutes. He glanced over to me and said, "That horse has a broken leg." Then he strolled away. His criticism didn't sit well with me. I'd worked really hard to put this show together, and that cowboy shot me down with six simple words.

Even at that young age I realized his criticism was accurate, and I had a lot more hard work in front of me if I wanted to be successful as an artist. Realizing I couldn't do it alone, I sought help. I worked and lived with working cowboys and participated in artist workshops put on by nationally known professionals. My "good work" as an artist was being perfected—and still is to this day. It is much the same as God continuing His good work in me through the Holy Spirit. Jesus said:

> Truly, truly I say to you, he who believes in Me, the works that I do, he will do also; and greater works than these he will do; because I go to the Father. Whatever you ask in My name, that will I do, so that the Father may be glorified in the Son. If you ask Me anything in My name, I will do it.
>
> If you love Me, you will keep My commandments.
>
> I will ask the Father, and He will give you another Helper, that He may be with you forever; that is the Spirit of truth, whom the world cannot receive, because it does not see Him or know Him, but you know Him because He abides with you and will be in you. I will not leave you as orphans; I will come to you. After a little while the world will no longer see Me, but you will see Me; because I live, you will live also. In that day you will know that I am in My Father, and you in Me, and I in you (John 14:12-20).

Jesus also said, "If you abide in Me, and My words abide in you, ask whatever you wish, and it will be done for you. My Father is glorified by this, that you bear much fruit, and so prove to be My disciples" (John 15:7-8). In those passages, it is clear to me that without the Helper in my life, I can't glorify God to my fullest capability. I've tried in the past to control my business and personal life and failed miserably according to God's standards of bearing the fruit of the Spirit.

Whatever made me think in the first place that I could honor God and help expand His kingdom without allowing His Helper to live and work in my heart? How did I get to a point where I didn't understand God's plan for my life? I'd grown up believing in the Holy Trinity—the Father, the Son, and the Holy Spirit as One. Did I buy into the worldview that since Jesus returned to heaven we've been left on our own until we die or He comes again to take us home? That we are forced to carry our burdens alone? I'm not sure. Perhaps it was a gradual erosion of faith.

I do know that the Helper is here to live and breathe and speak to us. He works in us and through us. What an honor to be an extension of God on this earth! I am able to proclaim the superiority of living every day with the Prince of Peace glorifying God through me as long as I submit to Him and listen for the voice of His guiding Spirit. This has been the plan for my life (and yours) since the beginning. Although it is a simple one on the surface, this covenant requires commitment. The ultimate sacrifice was made by the Father and the Son so we can be led by the Spirit of the living God, so we can experience a joyful and fruitful life designed for God's pleasure and glory.

All that we are and do should point to the One who spoke the universe and life into existence. God loves us so much that He chooses to care for us and provide for all of our needs. He does this even though we fall far short of His glory. As the apostle Paul wrote, "All have sinned and fall short of the glory of God" (Romans 3:23). I've spent a large part of my life giving only a small portion of my heart to the One who sacrificed everything for me. Yet through all I've experienced—my disappointments and failures—He's never left me. Instead, He stood beside me, waiting for me to turn to Him even more. He's continued to bless me and remain true to His promises. Now I'm embracing His truth heart and soul, choosing to walk in the knowledge and freedom of the Holy Spirit. I want to bear much fruit for God!

These words from The Message beautifully sum up my attempts to thank God for loving me, saving my soul, and giving me the greatest family and life a person could ask for:

> When the Friend comes, the Spirit of the Truth, he will take you by the hand and guide you into all the truth there is. He won't draw attention to himself, but will make sense out of what is about to happen and, indeed, out of all that I have done and said. He will honor me; he will take from me and deliver it to you. Everything the Father has is also mine. That is why I've said, "He takes from me and delivers to you" (John 16:13-15).

I remember being a young child of three and an extremely large hand with really big, scar-covered knuckles extended toward me from above. As I gazed upward, unafraid, and looked toward the bright morning sky, I saw a gentle, smiling face with loving eyes gazing down into my eyes. It was my granddad atop his bay horse, Old Dan. I was wearing a new white cowboy hat, leather vest, chaps, silver spurs, and Roy Rogers gloves with long black fringe. I sported a six-gun in my holster and had a sheriff's badge pinned proudly to my chest. Granddad was dressed much as he usually was at the turn of the century while riding up the Chisholm Trail. He was a real cowboy. It was the finest hour in my entire three years of inhabiting this planet. I had a grin from ear to ear to prove it. Wow! I was a real cowboy too.

It was rodeo time in Snyder, Texas! I grabbed that big hand and Granddad hoisted me onto the saddle behind him to ride down Main Street in the parade. I can remember hanging on to his belt with one hand while smiling and waving to all the people lined up along the street to watch the horses, wagons, and marching bands. I was certain that everyone came to see me in my new outfit and my granddad. I waved until I thought my arms would fall off. All the while, Granddad calmly guided Old Dan down the brick streets. When I got a tad too exuberant with my waving, his hand would reach back and grab me on the leg, steadying me as I rolled from one side to the other, basking in my newfound glory. When I got too out of control, he calmly said, "Easy, son. Be still." At the end of the parade I barely remember Granddad's gentle hand passing me down to my mother. I was half asleep from the grueling 17-minute ride.

Can you see a picture of the Holy Spirit in my granddad's actions? The Holy Spirit gently takes us by His hand of experience, not drawing attention to Himself but with a gentle touch and a still small voice He holds us in place, speaks the truth and will of God, and guides us safely forward. If there is one thing we as Christians all recognize, it is that we are loved completely and unconditionally. The Holy Spirit takes the very best, which is what God the Father and Jesus the Son offer, and gives liberally to all who believe and accept salvation through Jesus' sacrifice on the cross.

As I look back on that rodeo parade with my granddad, I can't help but be thankful for the love and kindness he showed me. I was so safe and secure. I felt such peace as I trusted the reins to his experienced and loving hands while reveling in the joy of the moment. My prayer is we will all learn to walk in that peace available to us through the Holy Spirit. Let us welcome Him as our ultimate Helper.

I've finally given up the performance mode of overachiever. It didn't produce good fruit or fulfill God's purpose for my life. I want the best God has for me! So I gladly choose to allow the Helper—the Holy Spirit—to take the reins and lead me down the trails He has chosen. I encourage you to do the same with this passage from The Message:

> God knew what he was doing from the very beginning. He decided from the outset to shape the lives of those who love him along the same lines as the life of his Son. The Son stands first in the line of humanity he restored. We see the original and intended shape of our lives there in him. After God made that decision of what his children should be like, he followed it up by calling people by name. After he called them by name, he set them on a solid basis with himself. And then, after getting them established, he stayed with them to the end, gloriously completing what he had begun (Romans 8:29-30).

Part 5

A COWBOY'S FAITH

Together We Can Make a Difference

Faith is confidence in what we hope for and assurance
about what we do not see. This is what the ancients
were commended for (HEBREWS 11:1-2).

When my grandson Jordan celebrated his fourth birthday, he was
really excited. For many days preceding the joyful event, he antic-
ipated with great enthusiasm all of the presents he would receive
from his friends and family. As we gathered around the picnic table in
the backyard with cake, ice cream, and balloons, Jordan was certain
of what was going to happen. Although he didn't visibly see the gifts
before the party, he was confident he was soon going to open lots of
presents, just like he did at last year's celebration. His faith was strong
because his previous experience had been a very real one. He was sure
of what he hoped for and certain of what he couldn't see. This is a wonderful picture of the simple faith God desires for all of us to have.

God made this hope available to every person more than 2000
years ago when He tore down walls that had divided nations from the
beginning of time. Jesus proclaimed, "A new command I give you:
Love one another. As I have loved you, so you must love one another.
By this everyone will know that you are my disciples, if you love one
another" (John 13:34-35). He prayed to His Father, "I have given them
the glory that you gave me, that they may be one as we are one—I in
them and you in me—so that they may be brought to complete unity.
Then the world will know that you sent me and have loved them even
as you have loved me" (John 17:22-23). This is the common ground
shared by those who believe in Jesus and desire to please God.

Faith, hope, and love are the threads that bind believers together.

While Christian unity doesn't allow for division, it does welcome variety. Paul tells us, "There are different kinds of gifts, but the same Spirit distributes them. There are different kinds of service, but the same Lord. There are different kinds of working, but in all of them and in everyone it is the same God at work" (1 Corinthians 12:4-6). He goes on to say:

> The body is not made up of one part but of many. Now if the foot should say, "Because I am not a hand, I do not belong to the body," it would not for that reason stop being part of the body. And if the ear should say, "Because I am not an eye, I do not belong to the body," it would not for that reason stop being part of the body. If the whole body were an eye, where would the sense of hearing be? If the whole body were an ear, where would the sense of smell be? But in fact God has placed the parts in the body, every one of them, just as he wanted them to be. If they were all one part, where would the body be? As it is, there are many parts, but one body (verses 14-20).

My friend Larry Randolph likes to refer to this description of the church as a galaxy of many planets revolving around the sun. We, as individuals of the great universe known as the church, must discover which orbit God has designed for us and then get into it. We should learn what our gifts are and then put them to use. When we attempt to be a part of the body we were not designed to be, we are out of our orbit and of little use to God. Unity is achieved when each part of the body functions as it was designed. Unity is the common ground we share to best fulfill our calling as members of the church.

We must accept the responsibility of our great calling. We need to not be content to sit idly by and allow others to do what we should be doing. Each part of the body needs to function as it was designed so we can reach many people with the wonderful news of Jesus. Working together, we can more effectively proclaim the message of hope that rests in the promises of our God and the sacrifice of His Son to die on the cross for us so that we can live forever in His glorious presence.

Jesus has sent us a Helper—the Holy Spirit—to give us the wisdom, strength, and passion to fulfill the great commission Jesus gave His followers: "Go and make disciples of all nations, baptizing them in the name of the Father and of the Son and of the Holy Spirit, and teaching them to obey everything I have commanded you. And surely I am with you always, to the very end of the age" (Matthew 28:19-20). We can experience the victory of walking in unity with the Almighty. We should approach opportunities to share our hope with the exuberance of a child opening presents at his or her birthday party. Salvation through Christ is the greatest gift anyone can ever receive.

> Lord, make us an instrument of Thy peace. Where there is hatred, let us sow love; where there is despair, hope; where there is sadness, joy; where there is darkness, light. O Divine master, grant that we may not so much seek to be consoled as to console; not so much to be loved as to love. For it is in giving that we receive, it is in pardoning that we are pardoned, it is in dying that we are born again to eternal life.
>
> ST. FRANCIS OF ASSISI

It is time to mobilize the body of Christ in unity to watch over and care for one another, to pray for and forgive one another, and to reach out in love and truth to people everywhere. In His faithfulness, God has provided a picture of a model church to help us understand our unity in Christ and our work in His name. Let's explore the pattern He reveals in the church at Thessalonica. And as we share this journey, I pray we will see and embrace our common ground consisting of peace, love, and hope. Let's witness God's love at work in the church at Thessalonica and see how He is still at work in our lives today. Together we can make a difference!

A Strong Foundation

My wife and I joined our three-year-old grandson as he said his prayers before bedtime. As he prayed, he tossed and tumbled across the bed the entire time, even performing a somersault at one point. Little boys often have difficulty being still, even when praying. We listened attentively as he finished blessing the entire family and were totally surprised when he closed with the Lord's Prayer. Much to our amazement, he didn't miss a single word or inflection throughout the entire prayer, despite his rolling and wiggling. When we asked how he'd learned to pray like that, he jumped up, blond hair projecting in all directions, pajamas twisted up, and replied nonchalantly, "My mommy taught me." The time our daughter had taken out of her busy schedule to teach her son how to pray had helped build a strong foundation in his young life. I decided moments like these are often life's greatest rewards.

Our lives are so full of distractions. It's easy to find a million reasons why we don't have time to read a Bible story to our children or attend a church function. But the rewards for obedience are so wonderful. When the apostle Paul established the church in Thessalonica circa a.d. 51, he was committed to establishing it on the strong foundation of Christ. During his second missionary journey with his companions Timothy and Silas, Paul took the time to write a letter to assure the church of his love. He praised them for remaining faithful despite being persecuted by the Roman government. He reminded them of the hope they had in the promise of their Savior's victorious return.

Thessalonica was similar to the large cities in today's world. It was a thriving seaport located on the most important highway that extended from Rome to the Orient. A wealthy city with a population of more than 200,000 people, Thessalonica was home to many pagan religions and various cultural influences that made professing belief in Christ dangerous...even life-threatening. Paul's letter commends the new believers for their faithfulness under such severe persecution.

In 1 Thessalonians 1, we see the origins of the rock-solid church in Thessalonica. Three elements come together to serve as the foundation: "Paul, Silas and Timothy, to the church of the Thessalonians in God the Father and the Lord Jesus Christ: Grace and peace to you" (verse 1).

First, we see the human element. Paul and his friends endured great hardship and persecution because of their faith in Christ. Even when their lives were in danger, they were not deterred in their efforts to fulfill the great commission of spreading the gospel throughout the world. Their attitude was one of obedience to Christ. How would people hear the gospel if Christ's followers didn't proclaim it? So they gladly accepted their position in the body of Christ and fulfilled their calling.

Second, we see the divine element. The church was established by God the Father and His Son, Jesus Christ. Paul explains that God chose to establish His church with His Word and the power of the Holy Spirit. People are only able to experience the power of the gospel of Christ when God reveals Himself through His Word. Lives are dramatically changed forever when God's Word is heard and obeyed (verses 4-5). Jesus emphasized that the power of the gospel is available to everyone: "Ask and it will be given to you; seek and you will find; knock and the door will be opened to you. For everyone who asks receives; the one who seeks finds; and to the one who knocks, the door will be opened" (Matthew 7:7).

The third element in the formation of the church was a blessing: "Grace and peace to you" (1 Thessalonians 1). Just as the Thessalonian believers were suffering from oppression and persecution, so many people today are starving for peace and rest in this hurried and chaotic world we live in. The typical family becomes weary just trying to cope with everyday life. When both parents have jobs and shuffle children between school, church, and extracurricular activities, stress and exhaustion become prevalent. Many young professionals are so consumed by their climb up the corporate ladder that their relationships become strained and their priorities blurred. Jesus said, "Come to me, all you who are weary and burdened, and I will give you rest. Take my yoke upon you and learn from me, for I am gentle and humble in heart, and you will find rest for your souls. For my yoke is easy and my burden

> Strength of character may be learned at work, but beauty of character is learned at home.
>
> HENRY DRUMMOND

is light" (Matthew 11:28-30). It is the responsibility of the church to share these valuable words and help create an oasis of grace and peace in our society.

The human and divine elements coupled with the blessings of grace and peace have been so important in my life. I was fortunate to have been raised in a Christian home where a strong foundation of faith was passed down from generation to generation. My parents and grandparents shared their faith freely and often and emphasized the importance of God's Word.

There is no greater responsibility or privilege than to build a strong spiritual foundation in our homes with our children and grandchildren. As the apostle Paul and the early church believers didn't yield to the dangers surrounding them, we too must not allow the busyness of our lives to interfere with our top priorities.

As we share the gospel with those around us, we give them the opportunity to experience the most life-changing event in history. The divine power of God in a person's life will replace fear, loneliness, and apprehension with grace, peace, and love. The Holy Spirit will bring guidance, comfort, and power in times of weakness and need. So many people long for peaceful rest. Like Paul, Timothy, and Silas, let's fulfill our calling. We can make a difference!

Three Keys to Success

Many American families endured extreme hardships during World War II. My uncle Raleigh Mason and his family were no exception. Like many young men during that day, Uncle Raleigh enlisted in the Army Air Force to defend our nation after the Japanese attacked Pearl Harbor on December 7, 1941. He was only 20 years old and had spent his youth helping his dad and brothers run the family ranch. As a young man, he'd heard the qualities of faith, hope, and love preached at home, in church, and at camp meeting revivals. These ideals became his most treasured possessions.

Prior to his deployment to Corsica, Raleigh became engaged to his high school sweetheart. Then they were separated by war. Uncle Raleigh flew more than 60 combat missions in Italy, Austria, and Yugoslavia, experiencing some close calls but sustaining no serious injuries. His last flight was on April 4, 1945, in Italy. His aircraft took a direct hit that destroyed an engine. The plane crashed in a marshy field, and the surviving crewmen were taken prisoner by the Italian army. They transferred the crew to their allies, the Germans. Each man was stripped of his insulated clothing and personal effects. Then they were forced to march to Austria. After that, the entire group was put on a train headed to a German prison camp near Munich.

When they arrived, they discovered many of the prisoners had been in the cold and damp prison for up to five years. Food was extremely scarce, and disease was rampant. Uncle Raleigh lost almost 50 pounds in two months and watched many of the men around him perish.

Meanwhile, his family had been notified of his disappearance and presumed death. It was a sad and somber time for many families in

America. All Raleigh's family could do was support each other in prayer and hope the war would end soon.

My uncle's faith in God gave him the strength to endure the tortuous months in the prison camp. His hope for survival was fueled by his love for his family and his sweetheart. Raleigh understood the power of faith, hope, and love. His willingness to sacrifice his life for others defined his undaunted patriotism.

After several grueling months in the prison, Raleigh knew his suffering was almost over when he heard that troops led by General George Patton were rolling in and freeing prisoners. The Allied Forces had prevailed! In just a few weeks Uncle Raleigh was back home, sharing the laughter of love and tears of joy with his family and friends. His faith and that of his family and friends had truly been tested. They had endured the hard times. The brave young soldier emerged from the perilous trials of war a more mature and faith-filled man.

Uncle Raleigh's hope was anchored to the promises of God, and his faith was truly rewarded. His sacrificial love for others was an example of what God wants all of us to have for one another. We can look to people who have exhibited the qualities of faith, hope, and love in their lives and see how the results produced endurance. The apostle Paul wrote, "We remember before our God and Father your work produced by faith, your labor prompted by love, and your endurance inspired by hope in our Lord Jesus Christ" (1 Thessalonians 1:3). These three characteristics—faith, hope, and love—comprise the common ground shared by all effective Christians.

The Thessalonian believers were people who were sure in their faith. Hebrews 11:1 tells us, "Faith is confidence in what we hope for and assurance about what we do not see." Since we've experienced the same revelation from God as they did, shouldn't we be operating in the same realm of faith? The writer of Hebrews added, "Without faith it is impossible to please God, because anyone who comes to him must believe that he exists and that he rewards those who earnestly seek him" (verse 6).

Today we find ourselves surrounded by a world with a faith often centered on scientific probability rather than divine revelation from God. If we are determined to make a difference, we must make sure our faith in God is not compromised.

The early Christians worked hard and persevered in the gospel because they had the love of Christ in their hearts. We all know that it takes effort to build and sustain relationships. Being totally honest, most of us will admit that we tend to love ourselves more than anyone or anything else most of the time. Jesus said, "My command is this: Love each other as I have loved you. Greater love has no one than this: to lay down one's life for one's friends" (John 15:12-13). Jesus gave His life so we can live eternally with Him in the presence of our heavenly Father. The majority of Christians in the early church were persecuted—sometimes even killed—for their beliefs. Even today many missionaries and believers across the globe face oppression and dangerous situations as they fulfill the great commission.

The steadfastness of hope allows us to endure. Let's face it—life is hard. We often ask ourselves if what we're doing really makes a difference. It's easy to get discouraged when we go out of our way to do something nice for someone and yet receive little or no thanks in return. When we are treated unfairly and things aren't going our way, do our reactions lean toward hope or hopelessness? James 1:2-4 offers some very encouraging advice: "Consider it pure joy, my brothers and sisters, whenever you face trials of many kinds, because you know that the testing of your faith produces perseverance. Let perseverance finish its work so that you may be mature and complete, not lacking anything."

If our hope is truly in God, then we will be able to endure anything life throws at us. God never promised us life would be easy. But He did promise to always be with us and to help us endure or escape life's difficulties: "No temptation has overtaken you except what is common to mankind. And God is faithful; he will not let you be tempted beyond what you can bear. But when you are tempted, he will also provide a way out so that you can endure it" (1 Corinthians 10:13). He wants us to be mature and complete because then we experience His joy and are of the most use to Him.

The Power of the Good News

Watching my grandson Hunter play in his first baseball game, I couldn't help but observe a spiritual picture of the way God works in our lives. Hunter's team is made up of four-, five-, and six-year-old boys and girls whose exuberance for the game is explosive and, as you might guess, rather clumsy and even comical at times.

Before the game, the players went on the field to practice—running, jumping, and often tripping over their own feet or those of their teammates. With caps tightly pulled down over their eyes and gloves in place, they played catch. Some would throw the ball to the wrong player, often hitting a teammate in the head or leg. Others squatted and made designs in the sand with pebbles and blades of grass, forgetting altogether why they were there. The coaches were continually trying to get the players to focus on the game, but the youngsters' attention spans didn't afford much cooperation. Soon the pregame warm-up was over and the call "Batter up!" rang through the bleachers filled with proud parents and grandparents.

The players had all received the "good news" of baseball with great power. Each had practiced knocking the ball out of the park, running the bases, and sliding fearlessly into home plate in a cloud of red dust. But as the game progressed, it was evident by their indecisiveness and sloppy fielding that they really didn't understand the object of the game and the importance of knowing the rules. When a player finally retrieved the ball, he would hold it or struggle with his teammate over it, paying the runner no mind. If a plane or bird flew over the field, forget about baseball. All eyes were on the sky no matter what was happening on the field. A player might meet a pal from school playing

second base for the opposition, and the two friends would stop everything and run out into right field together while pursuing a butterfly.
On one hand, it was a hilariously good time. But as a granddad who
used to be a pretty good ball player, I found myself frustrated by the
players' performance, including my grandson Hunter's. Then I noticed
the coaches.

In this young age group, several coaches are allowed to be on the
field with the players to help them make decisions. I noticed that each
time a youngster made anything even remotely resembling a good
play—whether it was falling clumsily on top of the ball or chasing it
after it zoomed between their legs—afterward he or she was patted
on the back and congratulated. When the outfielder was gazing at the
plane up in the sky instead of at the batter, a coach gently tapped the
player's shoulder, whispering a reminder to pay attention. When someone cried because the wire catcher's mask was intimidating, the coach
hugged him and whispered something reassuring. Soon the catcher
was all smiles and taking to the dirt behind home plate. No matter how
poorly he or she performed, each player was assured that everything
was all right. Everyone received high-five votes of confidence.

Isn't that a lot like the life of a Christian? We accept the Good News
of the gospel and the power of the Holy Spirit in our lives. And then,
just when we think we are playing by the rules and really giving God
our best, we get distracted by the world around us and take our eyes
off the ball. But our Helper, who is with us as God promised, whispers
softly in our ear, convicting and correcting us while gently guiding us
back to the bases of Christian life.

The apostle Paul wrote, "We know, brothers and sisters loved by
God, that he has chosen you, because our gospel came to you not simply with words but also with power, with the Holy Spirit and deep conviction. You know how we lived among you for your sake. You became
imitators of us and of the Lord, for you welcomed the message in the
midst of severe suffering with the joy given by the Holy Spirit" (1 Thessalonians 1:4-6).

The word "gospel" is translated "Good News," and these Thessalonians truly believed and accepted the apostle John's admonition: "God

so loved the world that he gave his one and only Son, that whoever believes in him shall not perish but have eternal life" (John 3:16). The Good News regarding the death, burial, and resurrection of Christ for them came to them in power. Jesus promised:

> If you love me, keep my commands. And I will ask the Father, and he will give you another advocate to help you and be with you forever—the Spirit of truth. The world cannot accept him, because it neither sees him nor knows him. But you know him, for he lives with you and will be in you. I will not leave you as orphans; I will come to you (John 14:15-18).

When we believe and accept the gospel, a miraculous and marvelous event takes place. The Spirit of God takes up residence in us and moves graciously upon our hearts and consciences to reveal the very heart of God. Christ's death on the cross made a personal relationship with Him available to all who choose to accept His gift of salvation.

There is no greater common ground among believers past, present, or future than our privilege of talking personally and directly to God. We are members of a team guaranteed victory. Our Coach has limitless patience and offers total forgiveness.

Imitators of the Lord

I learned so much about the value of good works when I was growing up by simply watching the man I knew as my dad. (My biological father was killed in a car crash before I was born.) To this day, he is the best example of faith in motion I've ever witnessed. I recall our long summer vacation drives across Texas to visit our family. Eight hours in a car with my little brother and me asking, "Are we almost there yet?" every five minutes almost drove my parents crazy. We were so anxious to see our grandparents and play with our cousins. Anything that slowed us down fueled incessant questions and complaints.

But Dad had other priorities. It seemed like a car or two was always broken down on the side of the road on our trips. Dad would pull over to render assistance. A great mechanic, Dad could fix almost anything. As my brother and I sat pouting in the hot car, Dad would climb under the other vehicle's hood, making adjustments with greasy wrenches and fiddling with steaming hoses for the driver of a pickup truck or hunker down in a ditch to change a flat tire for a lady stranded with her children. My brother and I waited in agony, just knowing we were never going to arrive at our destination. Eventually Dad, covered in grease, sweat dripping down his shirt, would silently climb back in behind the wheel and drive off. I never once heard him complain.

In the years to come, I accompanied Dad with a bag of groceries for a needy family someone had told him about. I watched him mow yards for widows and patch roofs and windows for neighbors after hurricanes. I saw him sit and talk to the lonely and heartbroken elderly in nursing homes, trying to bring joy into their days. I remember his late-night visits to the hospital, offering comfort to the sick and to their families. I heard his kind words of encouragement for the boys he coached on my Little League team and witnessed the time he took to teach and build confidence in each young player. I watched him share the delight of his grandson's birth and dry a mother's tears as she wept over her son's flag-draped casket just back from war. My friends, that is salt and light. That is a life modeled after our Lord. That is the role for all who are called Christians.

The apostle Paul encouraged the Thessalonian believers, "You became imitators of us and of the Lord, for you welcomed the message in the midst of severe suffering with the joy given by the Holy Spirit. And so you became a model to all the believers in Macedonia and Achaia" (1 Thessalonians 1:6-7). Despite persecution, often even to death, the believers in the early church were committed to being living examples of the gospel they had joyfully accepted. It is difficult for most of us to imagine how hard it was to model Christianity in a place where the government and people were so violently opposed to it. We are fortunate in the United States to have seldom experienced that extreme type of oppression. But when we take a broad, sweeping look at our society today, we see a spirit of hopelessness and cynicism that is very unhealthy. Apathy prevails where there is a lack of hope. The church must once again ignite in people the hope of victory through Jesus. Jesus painted a picture of how we, individually as believers and collectively as the church, need to make a difference in our communities:

> You are the salt of the earth. But if the salt loses its saltiness, how can it be made salty again? It is no longer good for anything, except to be thrown out and trampled underfoot. You are the light of the world. A town built on a hill cannot be hidden. Neither do people light a lamp and put it under a bowl. Instead they put it on its stand, and it gives light to everyone in the house. In the same way, let your light shine before others, that they may see your good deeds and glorify your Father in heaven (Matthew 5:13-16).

When a seasoning becomes flavorless, it is of no value to the cook. Likewise, when Christians are satisfied just occupying a pew week after week, making no effort to positively affect the world around them by sharing the joy of the gospel, they become flavorless and, consequently, of little or no value to God. Just as seasoning is necessary to bring out the best flavor in the foods we cook, Christians need to bring out the best in the people around us.

If you've ever driven a car at night across a vast, flat landscape in total darkness, it's easy to understand Jesus' analogy of a city on a hill. I've driven for several hours at a time across West Texas seeing no lights at all except what my vehicle was generating. Then suddenly the glow of a town appears on the horizon. It may be 50 or more miles away, but the radiance from the lights shining together is clearly visible. It is impossible to miss it. Jesus said that our lights as Christians should glow just as brightly so we can glorify our heavenly Father for all the world to see.

RE-READ - OFTEN

There are many ways we allow our lamps to be put under bowls. Sometimes we have an occasion to share our hope with others but choose to remain silent for fear of offending them by our faith. Sometimes we conclude that it's easier to go along with the majority and not make waves than it is to take a stand for what we know is right. Sometimes we don't stop to help others in need because it interferes with our own busy schedules. Sometimes we simply don't want to get involved. But God wants our lights to shine brightly so that others will see our good works.

The Thessalonians are good models for us to follow because they imitated Christ and were salt and light to their region of the world. Our lights grow dim and our faith weakens when we stop modeling the life of Christ. James explains how simply this principle is applied:

> What good is it, my brothers and sisters, if someone claims to have faith but has no deeds? Can such faith save them? Suppose a brother or a sister is without clothes and daily food. If one of you says to them, "Go in peace; keep warm and well fed," but does nothing about their physical needs, what good is it? In the same way, faith by itself, if it is not accompanied by action, is dead. But someone will say, "You have faith; I have deeds." Show me your faith

without deeds, and I will show you my faith by my deeds. You believe that there is one God. Good! Even the demons believe that—and shudder (James 2:14-19).

The common ground of responsibility for all Christians is to prove our faith by our actions. Helping others accomplishes two great things. First, it shares hope with those in need, thus glorifying God. Second, it strengthens our faith and fulfills our desire to please God. It makes us feel good to know that our light is shining for Christ.

The Pursuit of Excellence

More than 35 years ago, my grandmother gave me a short poem she'd cut out of the newspaper and placed in a small gold frame. It is now yellow and faded, but I still enjoy taking it off the shelf and reading it. I don't know who wrote the lines, but the author certainly understood the importance of Paul's words about respect.

YOUR NAME

It came from your father, it was all he had to give
So it's yours to use and cherish as long as you may live.
If you lose the watch he gave you, it can always be replaced.
But a black mark on your name, son, can never be erased.
It was clean the day you took it and a worthy name to bear.
When I got it from my father, there was no dishonor there.
So make sure you guard it wisely—after all is said and done.
You'll be glad the name is spotless when you give it to your son.

—Author unknown

While the poem has special significance for me in this physical world, I see a spiritual significance as well. Our very name, "Christian," came as a free gift from our heavenly Father. When He sent His only Son to die a lonely and humiliating death on the cross for us, He gave His most precious gift. "Jesus" is the name above all other names, and it should be used with all the gratitude and reverence we can express. We should cherish and honor Him as long as we live.

The apostle Paul advised, "We instructed you how to live in order to please God, as in fact you are living. Now we ask you and urge you in the Lord Jesus to do this more and more" (1 Thessalonians 4:1). If we could pray only one prayer a day, we would do well to say, "Lord, help me be more pleasing to You today than ever before." Our very reason for life is contained in that simple prayer.

God's desire is for us to continually strive to do better in our pursuit of excellence and holiness. The closer we walk with Him, the more He can use us to further His kingdom. Part of our sanctification process requires effort on our part to be more like Jesus. Paul urges us to "continue to work out your salvation with fear and trembling, for it is God who works in you to will and to act in order to fulfill his good purpose. Do everything without grumbling or arguing, so that you may become blameless and pure, 'children of God without fault in a warped and crooked generation.' Then you will shine among them like stars in the sky" (Philippians 2:12-15).

As we allow God to work in us, we share the common ground of fulfilling His purpose. Our pursuit of excellence will make us shine like stars! God seems to like things that shine, doesn't He?

Paul commends the Thessalonian believers for their love for each other, but once again encourages them to do so "more and more" (1 Thessalonians 4:9-10). Love makes our actions and gifts useful to God. Without love, the things we do won't have much impact.

> If I speak in the tongues of men or of angels, but do not have love, I am only a resounding gong or a clanging cymbal. If I have the gift of prophecy and can fathom all mysteries and all knowledge, and if I have a faith that can move mountains, but do not have love, I am nothing. If I give all I possess to the poor and give over my body to hardship that I may boast, but do not have love, I gain nothing.
>
> Love is patient, love is kind. It does not envy, it does not boast, it is not proud. It does not dishonor others, it is not self-seeking, it is not easily angered, it keeps no record of wrongs. Love does not delight in evil but rejoices with the truth. It always protects, always trusts, always hopes, always perseveres. Love never fails (1 Corinthians 13:1-8).

Paul also writes, "Make it your ambition to lead a quiet life: You should mind your own business and work with your hands, just as we told you, so that your daily life may win the respect of outsiders and so that you will not be dependent on anybody" (1 Thessalonians 4:11-12). I believe Paul closes this section of his letter this way to emphasize the importance of being a hard-working, well-respected member of society. If we win the respect of people, they are more likely to listen to us. If we are able to help others who are truly in need of assistance, we can demonstrate God's love to them.

Our loving God gives us many gifts in life. Because we are merely human, we sometimes don't recognize where they are coming from. We may lose them or squander them, but because He is always faithful and loving, He entrusts us with yet more gifts. When we are weak and stumble and cause a black mark to be placed on our names, He is faithful to erase it if only we'll ask.

Oh yes, our name "Christian" was clean when we got it! It was whiter than snow. A name that God said we who believe in His Son are worthy to bear. Our inheritance is the free gift of a spotless name washed in the blood of God's Son. That is the reason we pursue excellence. That is our common ground.

Power to Endure

My grandmother was a pioneer woman in West Texas who bravely endured life's many hardships and heartbreaks. Through faith and hope in God, she lived her 84 years determined to let her light shine despite the disappointments of this life. She never let her eyes stray from the reward that was to come. She dressed every day in the armor provided by God.

During her lifetime, my grandmother raised five children—three boys and two girls. Her first son died at the young age of 11 from polio during the epidemic that spread uncontrollably across America. A few years later, the Great Depression hit the people of Texas hard, and families struggled just to survive. Money and food were scarce, but my grandmother's family pulled together with neighbors and friends, sharing vegetables from their gardens and prayers of encouragement. Grandmother sewed many of her family's clothes from discarded cotton flour sacks.

During these trying years, her youngest son, Bill, was diagnosed with a severe learning disability. The schools were not equipped to care for him, so he remained at home and was nurtured by his mother full-time, as he would be throughout his life. Their family of six shared a small, one-room frame house that was held together by little more than the lumber of love and nails of hope. My grandmother endured life's hardships by trusting in the promises of God and being determined and ever hopeful.

The post-Depression years saw cotton become king in Texas, bringing new opportunities to many families. My grandfather seized the chance to start a business storing, testing, and shipping the crops raised by the farmers in the area. Grandmother, Bill, and the eldest son, Jack, all pitched in, and the business soon prospered. It wasn't long before they added a much-needed kitchen, a bathroom, and two bedrooms to their humble frame house. But just when life was finally going their way, the country entered World War II. Jack found himself in the perilous invasion of Normandy while his two brothers-in-law entered the service as pilots. Grandmother always attributed their safe return to four years of answered prayers.

Soon after the war, Jack returned home to work with his dad and expand the family business. Jack married, and the family was happier and more optimistic than ever, enjoying the post-war prosperity in America. The good times would soon end in another devastating tragedy for my grandmother. Jack and his young bride were involved in a terrible car accident. Jack didn't survive, and his expectant wife (my mother) narrowly escaped with her life and that of her unborn child. I was born six months later, bringing the hope of new life into the midst of this tragic time.

Within a few years, my grandfather died unexpectedly, leaving my grandmother alone for the first time in more than 55 years to care for her constant companion and youngest son, Bill. Despite all of life's disappointments and heartaches, Grandmother remained full of hope and optimistic about the future. She was a true inspiration to a lot of people, including me.

I considered Grandmother my best friend. I learned a great deal about faith, hope, and love from the many experiences we shared. We visited each other often, and, with Bill at our side, we fished many stock tanks and creeks in West Texas for catfish. We searched for Indian artifacts along the banks of the river and explored old abandoned barns and farmhouses while enjoying being together in the beauty of God's creation.

During our outings, Grandmother loved to share family stories, remembering all of the good times. Her face would glow as she recalled some 50-odd years in the past when her first son was so brilliant in math—the smartest boy in the one-room schoolhouse—before polio took his young life. She smiled ear to ear when she described how excited Jack was to receive her homemade cookies and bottles of Coca-Cola while dodging the bombs and bullets of the enemy. It made her proud that he always shared them with his buddies in his battalion.

Just prior to my grandmother's death, something very special occurred. I sat throughout the night next to her hospital bed as she slumbered peacefully. When she awoke the next morning, she shared with me a dream she had about heaven. Her face glowed with joy as she described the incredible light that surrounded her loved ones as she approached them through the clouds. Her husband, her two sons, her father and mother, and her brothers and sisters who had gone on before her were all there to welcome her with open arms

> Anything large enough for a wish to light upon is large enough to hang a prayer upon.
>
> GEORGE MACDONALD

and smiling faces. She had heard the call of the archangel. God, in His graciousness, had given her a glimpse of her imminent reward. In a few short hours, her dream became reality.

The light of hope that permeated my grandmother's life is the common ground of victory shared by all who believe in Jesus Christ and are called according to God's purpose. This is the hope that must be proclaimed with voices of unity.

Paul offers a description of Christ's victorious return to earth to claim His bride, the church. These words of encouragement are for believers throughout the ages. Paul explained how the same love that unites believers in this life will unite believers at the second coming of the Lord:

> The Lord himself will come down from heaven, with a loud command, with the voice of the archangel and with the trumpet call of God, and the dead in Christ will rise first. After that, we who are still alive and are left will be caught up together with them in the clouds to meet the Lord in the air. And so we will be with the Lord forever. Therefore encourage each other with these words (1 Thessalonians 4:16-18).

All Christians, either living or dead when Christ returns, will rise to live with Him forever! When our loved ones die, we should not despair. When world events threaten us with tragedy and hopelessness, we need to remember God's promises. He will transform death into everlasting life. He will turn tragedy into triumph, sickness into perfection, and hopelessness into eternal security in Him. He never promised us that the life we've chosen in Him would be easy, but He gave us those powerful words of comfort and reassurance so that we might share our hope with a hopeless world. This is the common ground of every believer.

Paul calls Christians to be ready for the unexpected and sudden return of Christ. So often we live as though there is no anticipation of the Lord's imminent return. Yet He will return, and no one knows the hour:

> The day of the Lord will come like a thief in the night. While people are saying, "Peace and safety," destruction will come on them suddenly, as labor pains on a pregnant woman, and they will not escape. But you, brothers and sisters, are not in darkness so that this day should surprise you

like a thief. You are all children of the light and children of
the day. We do not belong to the night or to the darkness.
So then, let us not be like others, who are asleep, but let us
be awake and sober (1 Thessalonians 5:2-6).

Wouldn't it be great if we all lived each day fully prepared for Jesus'
return? We can!

Paul reminds us of the spiritual armor we have been issued to help
us be prepared and endure the hardships of this life: "Since we belong
to the day, let us be sober, putting on faith and love as a breastplate,
and the hope of salvation as a helmet" (1 Thessalonians 5:8). Paul's ref-
erence to our armor is more thoroughly explained in his letter to the
believers in Ephesus:

> Put on the full armor of God, so that when the day of
> evil comes, you may be able to stand your ground, and
> after you have done everything, to stand. Stand firm then,
> with the belt of truth buckled around your waist, with
> the breastplate of righteousness in place, and with your
> feet fitted with the readiness that comes from the gospel
> of peace. In addition to all this, take up the shield of faith,
> with which you can extinguish all the flaming arrows of
> the evil one. Take the helmet of salvation and the sword of
> the Spirit, which is the word of God (Ephesians 6:13-17).

As we prepare for Christ's return, we must depend on God's
strength. He has given us the power of the Holy Spirit living in us and
every piece of armor we need to stand firm. It is our choice, however,
whether we choose to dress in the armor each day and experience victory or if we choose to settle for something less.

God wants us ready, and He promised that the gates of Hades
would not overcome His church (Matthew 16:18). When Christ
returns, the church is guaranteed victory. God wants us to wear His
armor until that day and share the common ground of victory filled
with courage and hope. As we endure this life on earth in the victory of
the Lord, the light of our hope will shine for all to see.

— 40 —

Encouraging Words

A few years ago, I joined some men in a prison ministry to share the gospel at one of our state's maximum security facilities. If anyone ever needed encouragement, it was these prisoners. They seldom— if ever—had any visitors, and most were very dejected and hopeless. I was somewhat apprehensive to talk with the prisoners, so at first I accompanied a friend who had been there before to get accustomed to the procedures. Prison can be a very intimidating place even for a visitor.

Later that afternoon I set out on my own, visiting with the men in solitary confinement. A guard opened the door to a long, narrow corridor, and I entered a block of eight cells. As the steel door slammed shut behind me, I suddenly realized I was alone with eight men who had been convicted of murder. I was consoled by the bars that separated me from the prisoners. Because I wanted to make the most of the short time I had been allotted, I immediately walked from cell to cell, speaking to each man. No one responded until I reached the guy in the seventh cell.

He was a large, imposing figure, standing about six foot four. He walked over to me and grabbed hold of the bars. "What do you want?" he asked in a low, monotone voice. I glanced toward the door at the end of the narrow hallway, hoping to be reassured of my safety by the presence of a guard. Realizing I couldn't see him behind the locked door, I looked at the prisoner and told him I was just there to talk and be his friend.

"Nobody ever comes in here to just talk," he said. He walked over to a small table beside his bed, picked up a crumpled, yellowed newspaper

SHARE/ WALK IT OUT!

article, and brought it to me. He handed it to me. As I began to read, I learned this man had been convicted for the deaths of his mother and his girlfriend. If he was trying to shock me, it was working. This wasn't what I was prepared for. "I ain't got no friends," he said as he hung his head. I was at a loss for words. What do you say to encourage someone who has committed such horrible crimes? After a moment, I replied simply, "I am your friend, and God is your friend. He loves you."

As the prisoner slowly glanced up at me, tears streamed down his face. We talked for almost half an hour as I presented the gospel and answered his questions about forgiveness. Just before I had to leave, we prayed together. He repented of the terrible things he had done and invited Jesus into his heart.

I never saw or heard from him again. I was given that one chance to encourage him. I do know he had new hope in his heart and a smile on his face when I was summoned back down the long, narrow corridor. I will never forget the echoing sound as the steel door slammed shut and locked behind me as I left.

Paul tells the Thessalonians, "Encourage one another and build each other up, just as in fact you are doing" (1 Thessalonians 5:11). This brings to mind a marathon runner who collapsed in total exhaustion prior to crossing the finish line. With the cheers and encouragement of friends on the sidelines, he somehow got up and mustered enough energy to finish the race. A word of encouragement at just the right time can change impending defeat into certain victory.

Closing his first letter to the Thessalonians, Paul lists 16 ways to share the common ground of encouragement with others:

1. "Build each other up" (5:11). Look for ways to encourage and support others. Let them know the qualities you appreciate in them. Help them with your words and actions.

2. "Acknowledge those who work hard among you, who care for you in the Lord and who admonish you" (verse 12). Look for ways to serve in your church and to cooperate with your leaders.

3. "Hold them in the highest regard in love because of their work" (verse 13). Support them with your appreciation. Let your leaders and coworkers in the Lord know how much their leadership, teaching, and hard work help you and your family.

4. "Live in peace with each other" (verse 13). We don't agree with each other all of the time, but we need to respond to others in love rather than react out of self-centeredness. We must find ways to work out our differences and come together, united in Christ.

5. "Warn those who are idle and disruptive" (verse 14). Those who are satisfied to simply fill a seat and not actively participate in the church need to be encouraged to use their talents. Invite them to help you in a project or service. Warn those who hamper the work of Christ that they aren't being all God designed them to be.

6. "Encourage the disheartened" (verse 14). Some people lack confidence due to inexperience or they may be idle due to shyness. If they have a willingness to serve, help them understand that God's promises are for them too, and that the body of Christ (the church) is not complete without them. Model ways in which they can participate.

7. "Help the weak" (verse 14). Be a friend to the weak and encourage them with kind words and actions. Pray for them, give them support, and let them know you care about them.

8. "Be patient with everyone" (verse 14). The fact is that some people really try our patience. In these instances, we need to remain calm and respond out of love rather than react from our self-centered points of view. We are all different, and we too engage the patience of others at times.

9. "Make sure that nobody pays back wrong for wrong" (verse 15). Sometimes we feel like getting revenge when we've

been mistreated or wronged. But Jesus said to do good to those who wrong us. Vengeance belongs to the Lord. Our command is to love one another as God loves us (John 13:34).

10. "Rejoice always" (verse 16). Even in the midst of life's troubles and heartaches, we can rest assured that God is in control. He has promised that all things work together for good for those who love Him (Romans 8:28).

11. "Pray continually" (verse 16). God resides in every believer through the Holy Spirit. He is *always* with us to hear us and guide us and even help us pray. He desires open lines of communication with us at all times.

12. "Give thanks in all circumstances" (verse 18). If we are sure God is in control and if we allow Him to control our steps, it is easy to give thanks in every situation. If we are trusting in ourselves, it's often impossible to be thankful. Note that Paul wrote to be thankful *in* all circumstances not *for* everything that happens to us. Bad and evil things don't come from God, but when we find ourselves in those circumstances, we can thank God that He is with us and that He will accomplish good things even in bad circumstances.

13. "Do not quench the Spirit" (verse 19). The power of the Holy Spirit in our lives provides the blessing of hearing from God and receiving our individual gifts and abilities. Paul tells us that when the Holy Spirit nudges us to do or say something, we should not ignore the instruction. This is the way God accomplishes His works through us, and it is critical that we cooperate with Him.

14. "Do not treat prophecies with contempt" (verse 20). We should receive God's Word from those who speak for Him, but at the same time we need to be cautious and test everything according to the Scripture (Acts 17:11). If

we think we disagree with what someone says, we should first check the Word. We can then accept what is true and reject what is false. The Word of God is the ultimate test.

15. "Reject every kind of evil" (verse 22). The world tempts us in every way possible. We must focus on obeying God and avoiding situations that are certain to be temptations. This reinforces the need to be in constant prayer. When we find ourselves in tempting situations, we can immediately talk to God about it. We also want to steer clear of any actions or acts that dishonor God.

16. "May God himself, the God of peace, sanctify you through and through. May your whole spirit, soul and body be kept blameless at the coming of our Lord Jesus Christ. The one who calls you is faithful, and he will do it" (verses 23-24). To experience peace and victory, we cannot simply allow God to control a portion of our lives while we hold on to other areas. The process of sanctification requires our willingness to allow God to be involved in *every* aspect of our lives: spirit, soul, and body. God wants all of our lives, not just a couple of hours on Sunday morning.

It's important that we follow Paul's guidelines to support and build up each other. Encouraging words change lives. If we put these principles into practice, our lights will shine like cities on a hill. People will see our good works and want to know more about why we have hope in Christ. And God will be glorified. God wants us to encourage others as He encourages us. And He offers us the assurance of His love and care:

> "For I know the plans I have for you," declares the LORD, "plans to prosper you and not to harm you, plans to give you hope and a future. Then you will call on me and come and pray to me, and I will listen to you. You will seek me and find me when you seek me with all your heart" (Jeremiah 29:11-13).

God wants us to share our hope and our future with the people around us. While opportunities like visiting prison don't come along every day, each of us can share kind words that help to brighten the lives of people where we live and where we work. Here are a few ideas of things to say:

- "You really did that well. Good job!"

- "That was a great talk."

- "That meant so much to my family and me."

- "Thanks for teaching our kids in Sunday school. I know it takes real dedication."

- "Thanks for caring."

- "You certainly made my day!"

- "You're such a great mom!"

- "I've been praying for you."

- "Thank you."

- "You look great!"

- "I'm sorry. Please forgive me."

- "You are so smart!"

- "I love you."

- "God loves you."

Everyone needs to hear words of encouragement. Paul knew that life would be hard, and he emphasized the need to build people up. The world will be a much better place to live in if people are more uplifting and positive and less critical.

Friends, it's time to let our hope in Christ shine as bright lights. It's time to watch over and care for one another. It's time to pray for one another and to forgive one another. It's time to reach out in love and truth to people everywhere. It's time to put on the armor God has provided and walk in the strength of His power. As Christians, it's time to do everything more and more. That is our common ground. Together we can make a difference!

> So for now, Lord, just let me ride on the trails of this life
> Till my job on earth here is through
> 'Cause I'm as close to heaven as I'll ever be
> Till I ride that great trail home to You.
>
> JACK TERRY, "Just a Cowboy"

JACK TERRY
Celebrated Artist and Author

**Granddad rode up and lifted me up on his horse Old Dan.
Right then I became a cowboy.**

I was inspired by my grandfather, a cowboy who rode on some of the last great cattle drives of the West; my grandmother, who painted the landscapes and people of West Texas; and my mom, who also enjoyed painting. I began my art career as a young child. With much encouragement from my parents and fam-

ily, I pursued my dream of being a Western painter. Cowboys and canvases were my passion, and by the age of 16 I'd won more than 130 awards in art. At 26 my big break came, and I was named Bicentennial Artist of Texas and commissioned to paint a portrait of the late President Lyndon B. Johnson.

I was taught "You got to live it to paint it." I've been incredibly fortunate to experience the cowboy life up close. I've spent many, many hours in the saddle riding the hills looking for cattle and enjoying God's great creation. On trail drives moving cattle, round-

ups, and the full-blooded experience of seeing some of nature's magnificence from horseback are what moves me.

I've had wonderful opportunities to pursue friendships and received one-on-one inspiration and training by many great painters. Because of their influence, my pictures span from historical moments in the American West to Victorian images, from landscapes to portraits. Talking with my paintbrush and taking people to breathtaking moments through canvas are my passions.

For information on my paintings, books, and more, please go to my website:

www.JackTerryArt.com

HORSE TALES FROM HEAVEN
Reflections Along the Trail with God
REBECCA E. ONDOV

Time to Hit the Trail!
Gifted writer and avid horsewoman Rebecca Ondov invites you to experience life in a wilderness horse camp. Drawing on 15 years of living "in the saddle" while guiding pack trips and working as a wilderness ranger, Rebecca shows you how the outdoors will open your heart and mind through true stories about...

- a frisky cayuse and an early morning chase
- the special friendship between a night-blind horse and a mule
- snoring at base camp—and a startling cure

Horse Tales from Heaven captures authentic Western life and reveals how God gets involved when you hit the trail with Him.

HEAVENLY HORSE SENSE
Inspirational Stories from Life in the Saddle
REBECCA E. ONDOV

Adventures in the Saddle
Horsewoman Rebecca Ondov takes you on some amazing pack trips in Montana's Bob Marshall Wilderness. Drawing on her years of working horseback, she takes you into the mountains to discover the unique personalities of horses and mules, the beauty of God's creation, and the wonders—and dangers—of nature. You'll experience...

- how a horse's amazing gift demonstrates God's provision and guidance
- the ingenuity of a mule that reveals a strategy for handling trouble
- a newborn filly's playfulness that demonstrates God's desire for relationship

Along the trail you'll encounter God's amazing love and the wisdom He offers if you'll only ask.